101
WAYS TO HAVE
A BUSINESS
AND A LIFE

ALSO BY ANDREW GRIFFITHS

101 Ways to Market Your Business
101 Ways to Advertise Your Business
101 Ways to Really Satisfy Your Customers
101 Ways to Boost Your Business
Secrets to Building a Winning Business

COMING SOON

101 Ways to Succeed at Network Marketing

101
WAYS TO HAVE
A BUSINESS
AND A LIFE

ANDREW GRIFFITHS

ALLEN&UNWIN

First published in 2007

Allen & Unwin
83 Alexander Street
Crows Nest NSW 2065
Australia
Phone: (61 2) 8425 0100
Fax: (61 2) 9906 2218
Email: info@allenandunwin.com
Web: www.allenandunwin.com

National Library of Australia
Cataloguing-in-Publication entry:

Griffiths, Andrew, 1966- .
    101 ways to have a business and a life.

    Bibliography.
    ISBN 978 1 74114 787 2.

    1. Quality of work life. 2. Work – Psychological aspects.
    3. Work and family. I. Title.

306.361

Set in 12/14 pt Adobe Garamond by Midland Typesetters, Australia
Printed in Australia by McPherson's Printing Group

10 9 8 7 6 5 4 3 2 1

Contents

Acknowledgments

As my life keeps getting busier by the day, I realise there has never been a better time for a book like this. In fact, I recently made the comment at a keynote presentation that I couldn't wait to finish writing *101 Ways to Have a Business and a Life*—because I really need to read it.

I could write a book to thank all of the people who have continually supported my writing and business career, but instead I hope I tell you often how much I appreciate everything you do. To Allen & Unwin, you are truly exceptional people and publishers. Thank you Ian, Carolyn, Andrew and Clara.

But as this book is about my journey towards and experiences with finding balance I have to thank a few people who have played a major role in keeping me on the planet a lot longer. First, Jenny Hayes and Louise Nelson, owners of Emerge for Life Health Centre in Cairns, who got me started on the journey that changed my life. Then there are my two amazing personal trainers, Sammy Slade and Kelly Sinclair, who have helped me lose a lot of weight, climb mountains and lift heavy things over a number of years—in spite of countless excuses from me, all of which were completely ignored.

Last, but not least, to Dr Debra Ruth Lawson, thank you for reminding me to love what I do.

Introduction

Why write a book about having a business and having a life?

The inspiration to write a book to help business owners find some balance in their overcrowded lives came to me from two equally significant sources. I am sure that since you are reading this book and clearly looking for a few answers, what you find here will ring true for you in some shape or form. Rest assured, you are definitely not alone.

The first source of inspiration is the sheer number of business owners I meet who feel that finding some kind of balance is the biggest challenge they face. I have done training seminars, sat on panels, been interviewed and conducted keynote speaking events on the topic. However, it never ceases to amaze me when I look at an audience and see the almost desperate look crossing hundreds of faces when the possibility of having a life *and* a business is tantalisingly introduced.

There was a time when just running the business was challenge enough. Today that is only a part of the problem, for trying to have a life as well as a business is increasingly a much bigger issue. Without doubt, when I ask business owners if they could have one thing, right here, right now, the answer is almost always the same: 'I wish I had a life.' How crazy is this?

So now you know—if you feel like this you are not alone, and that in itself is important. In this manic, intense world of ours, where there are a dozen ways to communicate with everyone else and expectations are higher than ever before, it's easy to see how we can lose control of our lives and get sucked into the vortex.

The second source of inspiration was the difficulty I had myself faced in doing the same juggle and dance. While I have for a long time now battled with finding any kind of balance in my life, I arrived at a real low point about five years ago.

I had never been busier, had as many obligations and commitments, or fought harder to keep some kind of sanity in the craziness that was my daily life. I was running a marketing company with lots of clients, writing books, sitting on company boards, working for charities, mentoring other business owners and generally making sure every minute of every day was full.

I had workaholic tendencies (OK, I was a workaholic!) that saw me starting at the office around five in the morning and working through till eight or nine at night, seven days a week. I lived like this for so long I forgot any other way of life. Looking back, it was ludicrous and sad. At the time I paid a heavy price, physically, emotionally and spiritually, but I hid behind the long-suffering business owner's belief that running a business was supposed to be all-consuming and that really, you didn't get to have a life because small business owners don't. I wore these beliefs as a badge of honour. Other business owners would sympathise with me over just how tough it was to run your own business and how, if you weren't putting in at least 80 hours a week, you really weren't serious about the whole thing. And I believed and helped to spread this propaganda.

In my most out-of-balance stage, my weight ballooned and I put on over 50 kilograms. I never exercised, I ate poorly, my marriage broke down and my friends stopped calling because I was always too busy to talk to them. The turning point came when my sister died suddenly from a heart attack at the age of 35 (I was 33 at the time). This shocked me into realising that the life I was leading was going to kill me. My doctor, my wife, my friends and even my clients were all telling me the same thing. Old habits die hard, however, and even though I realised that my life had to change I didn't really know how to change it. But the shift had started.

Today my life is busier than ever. I have come to terms with what balance means to me (and it is a little different for each of us) and I know that it is something every business owner can achieve. I don't want to be a Zen Buddhist monk—I like a certain degree of stress and I do my best work when I am under pressure. I like the buzz of having a lot of projects on the go at once and doing exciting and stimulating work, but I realised that the one thing I really wanted to lose was the manic nature of my daily life. Now I understand that there is much more to life than work and how sensational it really is to be able to enjoy every aspect of my life equally.

I don't think there is any one simple piece of advice that will bring the balance and harmony back. Many small changes are required; basically it means reprogramming and refocusing to undo the bad habits that have been created often over many years.

Today I am healthier, happier, more successful and definitely achieving far greater results in every aspect of my life. The day-to-day craziness has gone (most of the time), and I have a deep sense of calm and understanding that makes getting out of bed every day a delight. I get to face each day with a sense of anticipation and excitement that I had forgotten. And I like the way this feels.

So, my motivation in writing this book is to share some of the lessons I learned the hard way in the hope that you too can improve the quality of your life and your business. I believe that it is possible to have both and, if you can balance them and find your own sense of harmony, the end result is magnificently rewarding for you and for everyone you come into contact with.

But do I have all the answers?

When I was writing this book I knew that my experiences would be relevant to many business owners; however, I felt that I needed to draw on more experiences than my own. I discussed the concept of business–life balance with a host of business owners from around the world. I spoke to mothers in business, husband and wife teams, young entrepreneurs and veterans in the small business world. I have drawn on their experiences, challenges and advice in writing this book.

Based on this I address a wide range of topics, most of which are targeted at people who have probably already lost their sense of balance and are feeling totally overwhelmed— those of you whose businesses have taken over and who are searching for answers to get your lives back. This book includes everything from how we get out of balance in the first place to ways of retraining ourselves and those around us, the importance of what we eat and how we treat our bodies, and lots more.

If you are just getting into business and want to prevent yourself from getting out of balance, good on you for having the initiative to think ahead, because there is no doubt that this is a challenge you will face at some time. The very nature of small business makes it all-encompassing, wonderful, demanding, hard and rewarding. Being able to maintain a sense of balance and wellbeing while having your own business is a skill that will dramatically increase your chances of success.

What exactly does balance mean for you?

This is an important point, and I refer to it often throughout the book. Balance means something different for each and every one of us, and to find out what it means to you is the first step to achieving it. For some people it means no stress at all, having everything in perfect order, living a perfectly healthy life, feeling energised, calm and in control. For others it is cutting back the workday from 18 hours to 14 hours, the number of coffees from ten to five . . . You get the picture.

This is not a book about spiritual enlightenment, but a practical guide to help you find your own balance between your business and other aspects of your life. As you work through it you will form your own mental picture of how you would ideally like your life to look and feel.

What will you get out of this book?

Some of the benefits you will get from this book are tangible, others less so, but all are equally as powerful. These benefits include:

- a clear understanding of what balance means to you today;
- identifying exactly how out of balance your life currently is;
- gaining a very specific mental picture of how you would like your life to be; and
- simple step-by-step tips that will help you to make the changes that are necessary to embrace balance in your life.

The main reason nearly all of us struggle with business–life balance is that the changes which upset that balance occur slowly over time. They creep up on us, and all of a sudden we wake up and realise that we are out of control and we don't know what to do about it. That's exactly where this book steps in to help.

How do we know if our lives are out of balance?

This is a great question and one that we would all answer a little differently. Among the business owners I encounter, the most common response is an overwhelming feeling that they are no longer in control of their life or their business. They are being pulled in a hundred different directions, to the point where they just don't know how to break the cycle.

This feeling of being overwhelmed is probably the best indicator we have of being out of balance. We can feel overwhelmed by negative thoughts, negative people, circumstances and the long list of responsibilities we feel we should be meeting. Frustration, stress and often conflict outweigh the emotions of joy, peace, happiness and fulfilment. We have got so caught up in hectic daily activities, running on automatic, that at some point we have begun to question what it is all for. What am I doing with my life? What about me?

Being out of balance is a largely modern-day ailment that, if left undiagnosed and untreated, manifests as some of the more common health issues that seem to be occurring in plague proportions today.

The next section, How balanced is your life today?, contains a short questionnaire that will help you to work out where you are on the scale ranging from perfect harmony to completely out of control. It's a really great start to clarify exactly where you are at this time in your business life. If you repeat this questionnaire after following the tips in this book you should be sliding back down to perfect harmony in no time (well, that's the aim, anyway).

The top ten reasons for losing the battle of balance

The following list identifies the ten most common reasons for getting out of balance. While there are many more, these are the biggest culprits:

1. Overwork—simply putting in too many hours and being a slave to the business.
2. Financial problems—struggling to make ends meet in the business and worrying about how you will pay your bills.
3. Overcommitment—agreeing to do too much for too many people and not leaving enough time or energy for yourself.
4. Poor stress management—not knowing how to manage your own stress or not being able to admit that it is a problem.
5. Relationship issues—with partners, family and friends, co-workers and customers.
6. Poor lifestyle—eating badly, lack of exercise, and alcohol and drug abuse.
7. Lack of direction—feeling trapped and isolated in the business and uncertain about your future direction.
8. Lack of boundaries—being too accessible to too many people.
9. No space to rejuvenate—no holidays, time out, hobbies or distractions to remind you why you do what you do.
10. Having a negative environment or negative people around you every day.

Why do we get it so wrong?

Ironically, we get out of balance by trying to do what we think is right. We work hard, we commit completely to our businesses, we argue that to succeed we need to be devoted to growing the business, especially in the early stages, and, most significantly, we are energised and excited about the future.

Over time we get busier, our responsibilities grow and our needs and expectations are overtaken by the needs and expectations that others have of us. Then the feeling of being overwhelmed starts to move in.

The better you are at what you do, the more likely you are to start feeling overwhelmed—because more people want what it is you are selling. As your business grows there are more staff, more customers, more suppliers, bigger sums of money to manage and generally more paperwork to contend with. So in some ways, feeling out of balance with your business and your life is a reflection of the fact that you are great at what you do—take it as a compliment.

But before you get too carried away with patting yourself on the back and being proud that your life is completely out of control, remember that as your business has grown, you have had to learn a host of new skills to deal with this growth. Learning how to have a business and a life is just another set of skills that need to be learned along the way.

There are two ways to deal with being out of balance. The first is to change yourself and your perceptions. The second is to change your circumstances. Most likely both will be necessary. However you look at it, there must be a constant and ongoing commitment to do what is best for you, and the courage to create the necessary changes, so that you are honouring yourself, the people in your life, and the planet.

What are the long-term effects of being out of balance?

I can attest to the long-term effects of having a life out of balance—and they aren't pretty. The effects on health are the most noticeable, generally starting with headaches, skin conditions and an upset stomach, often accompanied by a general feeling of being unwell. Some people have a permanent cold or flu, get bags under their eyes or start to hear the comment, 'Gee, you look tired', a lot more often.

Along with the physical symptoms come the emotional ones. We start to get more irritable, we don't sleep as well as we used to, perhaps we start to get anxiety and even panic attacks, and we are irritable and generally highly strung. Under these conditions we can find ourselves leaning on crutches in the form of drugs and alcohol: after work we start to have three or four drinks to wind down; maybe we have three or four cups of coffee to get going in the morning. We eat chocolate to perk us up, which we need often because we have no energy, but which causes us to put on weight. Without making conscious decisions to change, and without knowing how to change, things will only get worse.

Of course, the longer you have bad habits, the harder they are to change and the more damage they can do. Business owners often tend to struggle the most with establishing a fitness and health regime, simply because they don't give themselves enough time or energy to focus on it. Someone who has a regular job generally has a start time and a knock-off time, and can more easily build a fitness program into their life.

What do you need to do right now to change the way things are?

Any change needs commitment. If you are desperate to make an improvement to your situation then you probably have the right amount of motivation. Without the right amount of motivation any change will be minimal and in all likelihood it won't last.

So right here, right now, you need to stop and think about just how important it is that you introduce some real changes to your life that will stop the feeling of being overwhelmed, and help you to start to take control of both your business and your life.

Think about how you want to feel, what it is that you want to do with your time, how you want to look, how you want to act and how you want to live your life. Once you are clear on this, or at least willing to start really looking at each aspect of your life, you can move on.

Remember that this is a journey—but it's not an overnight journey; it's about changing virtually every aspect of your life so that you can really get the most out of the years ahead. So there may be some pain, other people may not like the changes that you need to make, especially in the short term, and some may even try to sabotage the process (people generally don't like change, especially in those closest to them). This is where you need to be strong, dedicated and very clear on where it is you are heading.

How to get the most out of this book

We all have our own favourite method of reading a book, especially business growth books. Some people like to flick through the pages, stopping at the tips that strike a chord. Others like to start at the beginning and work their way from front to back in one sitting. The *101 Ways* series of books have all been written in a simple format that will work for both styles of reader. Open this book at any page and there will be tips, action points and things to do right now. How you use them is entirely up to your own needs at the time. My advice, though, is that at different stages in your life you will get different messages out of this book. Keep it handy, have an open mind and read it often to remind yourself of what you can do to find and, most importantly, keep balance and harmony in your life.

There is room at the end of each section to write notes and I encourage you to do this. Write whatever comes into your mind at the time. Trying to action each of these tips immediately is a hard ask. I recommend allocating time each week to making changes that will bring your life back into balance. It will be really rewarding—trust me.

At the end of the book I have included a list of excellent books that cover a host of related topics, as well as websites that will help you to win the battle of balance.

So without further delay, let's get started.

1 | How balanced is your life today?

Where are you at right now?

How do you know if your life is out of balance? That is a tough question for some people to answer. Life may be chaotic, but that doesn't necessarily mean that it is overwhelming—if you're like me, perhaps you like it that way. The following questionnaire has been designed to give you a simple way of determining where you are in the 'out of control cycle'. Simply put a tick next to the questions that you feel apply to you, then tally up the ticks and see the results.

The aim here is to have no ticks at all. Clearly a big ask even for the most serene and tranquil among us. Ideally, run through this questionnaire on a regular basis to see if you are regaining control of your life.

To make this exercise a little easier, I have included another copy at the back of the book. Photocopy it so you can ask yourself the same questions every couple of months to see if your life is improving.

How balanced is your life?

- ☐ Do you feel that you never have enough time to get everything done?
- ☐ Do you feel that your decision-making is always done under pressure?
- ☐ Are there times during your day when you feel totally overwhelmed or out of control?
- ☐ Do you think that stress is affecting your health?
- ☐ Do you always feel low in energy?
- ☐ Do you use drugs or alcohol to help you wind down?
- ☐ Do you use caffeine and sugar to help you wind up?
- ☐ Do you tend to eat foods that will give you a 'quick fix' rather than foods that are healthy and nutritious?
- ☐ Are you working longer and longer hours?
- ☐ Do you struggle to find the time to exercise?
- ☐ Have you stopped spending quality time with family and friends since starting or buying your own business?
- ☐ Have you stopped doing the things you love (hobbies, sport, etc.)?
- ☐ Do you tend to get sick more often or do you always feel off-colour/below par?
- ☐ Have you lost your sense of satisfaction with your business?
- ☐ Do you tend to keep your thoughts and emotions to yourself?
- ☐ Do you lose sleep worrying about business issues?
- ☐ Do you struggle financially?
- ☐ Has your personality changed (for the worse) since you've been in business?
- ☐ Have you stopped enjoying life as much as you did before?
- ☐ Are you feeling uninspired?
- ☐ Do you consider your time at home as being predominantly to recharge and prepare for the next day?

☐	Do you tend to feel negative more often than positive?
☐	Are you more grumpy and irritable now?
☐	Do you bring work home with you?
☐	Is every day starting to look the same?
☐	Do you have a lot of negative people in your life?
☐	Are you feeling depressed?
☐	Do you have a large number of unfinished tasks?
☐	Has your overall fitness level dropped in recent years?
☐	Have people stopped telling you that you look well?
☐	Do you sometimes feel like crying?

Total

How did you do?

21–31

OK, time to get serious and really look at your life. Balance is not a word that even comes close to being in your life right at this moment. If you don't make some changes now you will start to have major problems. Read this book and introduce the tips into your daily life at a pace that works for you. Many of the recommendations will bring instant results and you will regain that sense of balance before long. Start to enjoy the way this makes you feel and enjoy the benefits of regaining control of your life.

11–20

This is the middle of the road and typically where most people tend to hover. There are two ways to look at this: first, at least you're not as badly off as the first group; but second, the warning signs are clearly there that you may be on the way to a life of stress and all the issues associated with being out of control.

1–10
There aren't too many business owners who wouldn't say yes to at least a few of these questions. This is the best place to be, although it's important not to let things slide any further. You will be getting a few warning signs, probably a few symptoms of stress starting to creep into your life. Take heed and use these tips to nip them in the bud as quickly as you can.

0
You are a picture of pure tranquillity, you are Buddha personified. Throw this book in the bin or, preferably, give it to a friend who could really use it.

2 | Start the retraining process today

Most situations we find ourselves in that aren't to our liking generally haven't come about overnight. If we are really honest with ourselves, we probably knew they were happening but chose to live in denial until the situation got serious. We don't develop love handles over a weekend, but it's not until our clothes don't fit that we decide to join the gym and get moving. We don't generally max out our credit cards in one day either (although it would be easy)— they gradually climb, and we only take action when they are full, even though we well and truly knew what was happening.

The same is true of losing control of our lives when we become business owners. It starts innocently enough, then slowly but surely the business takes over and we lose control. We know it's happening but we kind of ignore it because we don't really know what to do. And, of course, it's only for a short while—everything will magically change back at some undetermined time in the future. We hope.

This section looks at starting the change process, determining your level of motivation and how you want your life to look and feel. Quite a few of the tips here suggest taking some time to write down your thoughts. Remember to take the time to do this as it is particularly beneficial.

#1   Decide right here, right now, if you are ready to change
#2   Take some time, alone, to reflect on where you are today

#1 Decide right here, right now, if you are ready to change

The first tip is the most important in this book. If you are not 100 per cent ready to wrest control of your life back from your business, you won't achieve it. I attended an interesting motivational seminar recently at which the host asked one man in the crowd of 4000 people what was wrong with his life. The hapless fellow rattled off a list of his woes, from no girlfriend to no money, niggling health issues but nothing serious, and a losing battle with his weight.

The well-known host, with a big grin, asked what was stopping him from getting his life together. The poor man gave a lengthy list of why he couldn't change any of the things in his life that he was unhappy with. They were all good reasons and they sounded reasonable to me, albeit a little defeatist and whiny. The host then said, 'If I gave you $1 million right here, right now, could you change your life immediately and rid yourself of the issues that are plaguing you and preventing you from making the most of your life?' In a heartbeat the man said, 'Absolutely—yes.'

Now this is interesting. It's not the problems or the solutions that are the issues. They are simply the mechanics of the situation. Any reasonably intelligent person can sit down and write a list of the issues that are affecting them and what they need to do about it, or find someone to help them do it. The secret ingredient to make change work is *motivation*. If you have the right motivation, you can change anything in your life. If you haven't, the change will only be token.

What can I do today?

Print or write this message on a piece of paper and put it on the wall, in your diary or wherever you will see it every day: 'I am taking control of my life back from my business. I am the boss.'

#2 Take some time, alone, to reflect on where you are today

Before you leap into action and start to change everything in your life, I suggest taking some time out to reflect on how your life is today, and how you *imagined* it would be. Some of it will be really on track, I am sure, but there are bound to be parts that are just not working for you.

In the normal state of craziness that most of us seem to live our lives in, there is little time to simply sit and reflect—but I think reflection is an incredibly powerful tool. To reflect on the journey that has got you to this point in your life means remembering the good and the bad, the dreams and the desires. To reflect on this means to take stock of where you are today, and this can really drive the change process because you will be motivated by remembering how you wanted your life to be.

There is a reason that meditation has become so popular in modern Western culture—remembering, of course, that it has been popular in some other cultures for thousands of years. (Perhaps we weren't that quick off the mark.) Quiet reflection is a form of meditation and it can do wonderful things for us if we take the time and create the right environment to let it happen.

So while I am recommending that you take time to reflect on where you are today, I also strongly recommend building time into your life for reflection *every* day—maybe at the end of the day, or maybe in the morning when you get up. It's up to you, but the things to think about are: How was the day you just experienced? What went well, and what didn't? What could you have done better? What are you proud of?

The funny thing about reflection is that you have to train your mind to do it; you need to ask the questions. In the early stages, think of four or five questions and ask them of yourself at your chosen daily reflection session. After a while, they will

START THE RETRAINING PROCESS TODAY

form in your mind automatically. It will be very calming and you will be better able to break your bad habits if you become aware of them on a daily basis.

What can I do today?

Give yourself time to sit and ponder, away from phones, customers, the family or any other distraction that will prevent you from being able to think clearly. Then just sit and reflect, maybe write down a few things that come into your mind. But generally just make peace with what has occurred to get you to this point in your life. Then make the time to do this on a daily basis.

#3 Understand the enemy—what things throw you out of whack?

If someone asks me what disrupts the balance between my business and my life I can easily list the culprits:

- Overcommitting my time (I can't say no and I get excited by interesting new projects).
- Aspects of running my company that I am no good at (bookkeeping, operational procedures, etc.).
- Day-to-day distractions that stop me getting my work done (I get hundreds of emails, countless telephone calls, letters, visitors, etc. every day).
- The internet—I love it and get distracted by it, and have to find the time to finish projects that I didn't get done because I was distracted (as you can tell I have a very short attention span).
- Poor time management.

That is me being perfectly honest about myself. I get lots done, I work long hours and I have very high expectations of myself, but the above issues bring me undone faster than any others. Fortunately for me I have a great team of people to work with; they are very aware of each of these issues and do their utmost to prevent them from impacting on me.

I suggest that you write your own list. What causes you the greatest frustration in your business? Is it worrying about money? Having to manage your staff? Is it caused by your suppliers? Or your customers? Again, try to be specific if you can. Often we haven't actually taken the time to think through the causes of our day-to-day angst. You can then start to do something about it and, even more importantly, you can enlist the help of those around you, who can generally see you slowly destroying yourself as you battle the panicky feeling of being overwhelmed by your business.

What can I do today?

Make a list of the issues that seem to cause you the greatest amount of grief on a daily basis. Once you have written it, put it in a prominent place and be committed to addressing these issues once and for all. Enlist the aid of others to help you.

#4 What bad habits have you developed?

The underlying cause of being out of balance is generally related to bad habits that have become part of your normal, day-to-day way of doing things.

These habits may relate to your health and wellbeing. Perhaps you eat badly because there isn't enough time in a seriously busy day to go that little bit further and get a healthier lunch. Or exercise consists of wrestling open a bag of chips, your only meal, sometime during the day.

Or perhaps you are drinking a lot of coffee to fight the fatigue of working longer and longer hours. Or maybe you are unable to make even simple decisions anymore simply because your mind is so full.

Whatever your particular bad habits are, rest assured, you are not alone. They come with the territory and I have had them all. I do know, though, that these bad habits will trap you if you don't act on them, and from my experience they are particularly hard to shift. Just like smoking, it's easy to start but amazingly difficult to stop.

Not all bad habits are obvious. It can sometimes be a matter of what you are not doing that is significant. Like not taking enough time to relax, not recharging your batteries by doing the things you love. These are generally by-products of the bad habits we have developed—but they should be listed as well to help you start the change process.

What can I do today?

Make a detailed list of all the bad habits that you have developed and the impact they have on you. Be honest, be specific and be prepared to be a little shocked. If you are not comfortable with this, don't show anyone else, but don't kid yourself either. Write them *all* down.

#5 Be clear about how you want your life to look and feel

Just as important as making the time to sit and reflect on your life as it is today is being clear on what you want your life to be like, or how you want it to look and feel, from here on.

I find that being clear about this makes everything else fall into place. The more specific you can be about how you want your life to be, the more likely you are to achieve it.

Often it is hard to be clear about just what it is we want out of life. Faced with a blank piece of paper, I struggled for a long time with my attempt to list how I wanted my life to look, or how I wanted my business or my body to look. I found it easier to write down the things I *didn't* want first of all—that made working out the things I *did* want much simpler.

Before I started my marketing company I had done a number of different things. I had been a commercial diver, run a small travel company, worked around the world as a sales professional, sold encyclopaedias door to door—and much more. I had reached a crossroad in my life where I was trying to decide what I wanted to do. So I wrote down all the things I liked about each of my previous professions, and all the things I didn't like, and from those lists determined what kind of business I wanted now.

The results were very specific. I had spent a lot of time working outdoors and being cold. Hence today I live in the tropics, but I didn't want an outdoors job. I used to be on call 24 hours a day when I had my travel company, but I didn't want to answer the phone at 3 a.m. anymore. I certainly didn't want to knock on doors to sell anything, but I did want to meet people and to travel.

What came out of the melting pot was a very clear set of criteria to be met by my next business—and that's how I came to be a writer and marketing consultant.

So when we are talking about regaining control of our lives and being able to successfully balance business and life, we need to know exactly what that means to us as individuals.

Writing it down makes it real. The form in which you do it—lists, tables, a flowchart—doesn't matter. Write down *exactly* how you want your life to look. Be very specific. Don't say you want to spend more time with your children—say how much more time. If you don't want to work as many hours, say how many hours you do want to work. If you want to earn more money, say how much. Specifics become reality. Airy-fairy, non-specific goals rarely get to be achieved.

The more specific your goals are, the greater your chances of making them a reality.

What can I do today?

Today is the day to make up the written picture of how you want your life to look and feel. Be specific, take your time—and keep your target list where you will always be able to see it.

#6 Old habits die hard—it takes time to change

While it is good to acknowledge that it has taken time to form the habits that prevent us from balancing our life and business, and that subsequently it will take time to change these habits, we need to get on top of the process of change and drive it.

This means that once all the distractions, bad habits, things that drive us insane, and anything else that can be blamed for throwing our lives into chaos are identified, we need to very deliberately set about changing them. Simply identifying the problems won't make them go away.

It is unlikely that we will change all our bad habits overnight. Everyone who has made a list of New Year's resolutions is familiar with the bitterness of defeat around 1 February when nothing has changed. We need to pace ourselves and plan to implement changes in a way that is manageable. Many of these changes may have an impact on other people, too, people who may need a little time to adjust accordingly.

We need to set up a time frame to change each and every bad habit that we've fallen into. Be reasonable—prioritise those that need changing soonest and set your time frame to achieve this. A day or a week, it's up to you. But put all these issues onto one piece of paper—again, put it in a prominent place and look at it every day.

Now you've followed tip #4 and tip #5, are you working towards making the changes? Are you on track timewise? If not, why not, and what do you need to do to get back on track? Understanding that if you don't change these issues your life will stay exactly as it is should be enough motivation to really get you moving. But the habits won't change themselves and some will be tougher to kick than others.

What can I do today?

Write the list, put a time limit on each and every issue—and make a mental commitment to meet every target.

15

#7 Develop your plan of attack and put it where you can see it

By now, we have achieved a number of key steps in the process. We have accepted the need to change, we have identified where we are going wrong, the bad habits we have formed and the daily distractions that stop us from being in balance. We have prioritised them, put time frames in place and been very clear on when we want these changes to be completed. The next step is determining what we need to do to make the changes happen. This is where we have to really spell things out. What *actions* do we have to take to make these changes happen?

An example that remains particularly vivid in my memory happened a few years ago. I had finally decided that I had to get fit and lose some weight. I was getting ever more seriously overweight and it was really only a matter of time till I dropped dead. (I had the right motivation.) So I made a list of all the things that stopped me from being fit, that made me put on weight and generally kept me in the shape I was.

Most of the things I wrote down were hollow excuses—no time, the business needed me or else it would fall apart, my clients would leave if I wasn't there to answer their calls from early morning till late at night, I was too busy to take the time for a proper lunch break so I ate on the run, and so on. In hindsight not one of them was true, but I had learned to believe my own propaganda.

Then I set my goals. They were big, but most of my goals are. I wanted to lose 50 kilograms and climb the tallest free-standing mountain in Australia (which is 922 metres—not Mount Everest by any means, but in my mind there was little difference).

Then I set time frames to achieve each of these goals. Three years to lose the weight (this was based on professional advice) and one year to be able to climb the mountain.

The next step was the action plan to achieve this. I went to a gym where a team of personal trainers started the process. They looked at my overall wellbeing, my goals and the reality of my situation. I was never going to be a beansprout-devouring kind of fella, so they developed a plan to suit me. We revised it often, always with my goals in mind. I pinned it up on my door at home, along with my goals, and I read both of them every morning as I walked out the door.

I am happy to say that both goals were achieved. For me, the biggest challenges in my life at that stage were overcome. I realised that I could apply the same simple processes to solving any problem, but specifically those that affected balancing my business and my life.

It is important to detail, step by step, the actions that you need to take to implement significant changes, otherwise they rarely happen.

What can I do today?

Write out your plan of attack in full and put it on the wall or somewhere you can see it often. As you achieve the tasks on the list, cross them off so you can keep track of the results you are getting.

#8 Start every day on the right path

I am a great believer in the importance of starting your day the right way. If you begin under the hammer, you will spend all day under the hammer. Taking some time each morning to start your day in a gentle, focused and balanced way lays the groundwork for the rest of the day.

I tend to spend a few minutes lying in bed, thinking about the day to come, getting my head ready and right. Or if it is a nice day I will sit on my balcony and watch the sun appear over the hills, and enjoy the sensation of warmth on my face. Whatever else happens, there is a definite relationship between the way I feel first thing and the way my day turns out.

I used to jump out of bed while it was still dark, gulp down some coffee, have a quick shower and head to work, where I was full-on from the minute I arrived until the minute I left, normally many hours later, in the dark at the other end of the day. This is a very stressful way to live—there is virtually no room to stop, breathe or enjoy what is happening around you.

Since I changed the way I start my day I definitely feel much better, more in control, more relaxed, and ready to take on the day and all its challenges in a calm manner.

This works for me, although I can't promise it will work for you. What is important is to start to bring a few rituals of relaxation into your life. They are going to remove the mayhem, ease the sense of being overwhelmed, introduce calm and allow clarity into your daily life, which will make you feel so much better.

What can I do today?

Plan to start tomorrow in a new way, to take some time just for you, to think about the day ahead, to visualise all the good things that will happen and the successes that you will enjoy. It really does work.

#9 Reward yourself for staying on track

One observation I have made of small business owners is that they generally struggle with the notion of rewarding themselves, often associating reward with purely financial considerations. Associated with all the changes we are talking about there can be more than a little turmoil in the short term before greater balance kicks in. This is normal, but the turmoil can be disconcerting, and we need to give ourselves some rewards along the way.

I suggest making a list (yes, I know, yet another list!) of things you consider to be rewards. Some may be material objects, others may be more symbolic. This doesn't matter— what does matter is that they are things you really like and want.

Add these rewards to the list of changes required to achieve your balance, at strategic places—so that when you change this habit, you get that reward. For example, your list might say that for one week you are not going to stay at work later than 6 p.m., no matter what. If you achieve this, your pay-off is to buy yourself a new fishing rod. Or, if you commit to going to the gym twice a week and you do it for a month without fail, you get to have a night out at your favourite restaurant. But you *must* make the change before you claim the reward.

This is part of the reprogramming process that you need to undertake. There are many names for 'reprogramming', and many ways to go about it, but it does work. We need to be rewarded—whatever that means to us individually—to really feel that what we are doing is worthwhile.

What can I do today?

Be clear about what you see as rewards, then make sure you give yourself these rewards as you achieve the goals and targets you have set. The rewards don't have to be huge, perhaps something as simple as taking time out to call a friend.

#10 Visit your doctor, healer or naturopath

A big component in achieving balance between business and life is being healthy. Stress encourages poor health and most business owners are under a lot of stress.

I suggest that you visit your chosen medical advisor and get a thorough check-up. Use it as a baseline. Where is your body at today? Whether mainstream or alternative (and best start with the mainstream if you are aware of anything significant, and even if you aren't), they will probably get you to have a number of tests, prod and poke you a bit, and give you advice that you don't want to hear, but the information will help.

Tell them that you are planning to make some significant changes in your life and this is one of the first stages. They may be able to recommend some professionals or organisations to help you.

I donate blood once a month, and have done so for almost 20 years off and on. I do this for three reasons: first, I get to lie on a bed for an hour and have a little quiet time, followed by a cup of tea, a biscuit and a chat to one of the lovely old ladies who looks after the donors. Second, it makes me feel that I am doing something good for society. Last but not least, I get a free check-up once a month. Before taking my blood they give me a fairly comprehensive physical that covers blood pressure, weight and various other things. If there is anything wrong it gets picked up quickly and lets me keep track of key health indicators. Occasionally I get a letter from the blood bank saying my last donation showed an issue that needs to be followed up; a quick visit to my doctor and all is well.

What can I do today?

Have a baseline physical done. This is another way of measuring the positive changes that occur with letting harmony find a way back into your life. You decide what type of advice you are after, but make an appointment for a complete check-up today.

#11 What are the things you have always wanted to do?

Make a list of all the things you have always wanted to do but have never found enough time, money or energy for. I find this a very interesting exercise. It's your 'life wish list', and what goes on it is entirely up to you. When we are feeling overwhelmed one of the biggest issues is that there doesn't seem to be any way out, that often there isn't a lot to look forward to except more of the same.

Having a list of things that you have always wanted to do (the 'one day I will' list) makes them more real. My list is long (about 30 items) and ranges from spending a month in India to feeling a polar bear's fur. I am glad to say that I have achieved a few of these things in recent years, and that feels sensational. Quite often I find more things to add—there are no hard and fast rules to this tip. It's your list—make it what you want. Sometimes you might even want to take a few things off, because as time goes by you can change and they may no longer be as important to you.

What you do with this list, like the others you make as you work your way through this section, is of course up to you. I made up a folder that holds all my information, and that works for me. I keep it handy and review it almost every day. Some of the more important parts I have laminated and placed on my wall. I don't care who reads them; in fact I find that it motivates my friends to get off their backsides and put their own lives into action mode.

Life is short, but we have the opportunity to do so much. By taking control of your life and putting your business back into perspective you will get to enjoy so many more of the amazing things this planet has to offer. Some are huge, some are small, but most are worthwhile. Running your own business is an amazing experience and provides a true sense of accomplishment, but this is magnified one hundred times if you can enjoy your social life at the same time.

What can I do today?

Make up your own list of things you have always wanted to do but have never had enough time, money, energy or courage to do. And then start working your way through them.

#12 Be prepared to invest in the process

To get back the balance that is missing in your life you will have to invest. This investment will be in the form of time, energy and money.

Part of your investment in time will be taken up when you sit and plan what you want your life to be like. Another part will be used to go to seminars, read books, talk to other like-minded people, to get fit, to learn better techniques for managing people, and for reflection. Time is our most precious commodity and the one most of us complain we don't have enough of. Of course, the old cliché is that we all have the same amount of time available (and I don't really need to talk about the likes of Bill Gates, Rupert Murdoch and Richard Branson all having the same amount of time as we do). Using your time to bring balance and harmony back into your life will reap great benefits for you and all those people close to you.

Your energy will be needed on a number of levels. You need energy to make the changes necessary to bring balance back to your life. You need energy to break out of the 'comfort zone' (the safety of the familiar) that tends to hold us in the state of being overwhelmed, and you need energy to keep going once you have made these breaks. The more successful you become in business the more opportunities and distractions come your way. Each one of them can play a role in throwing balance out the window. Energy is a powerful weapon in the harmony arsenal.

And last but by no means least is cash. You will have to invest in yourself in order to get fit, to reward yourself, to learn new skills and to change the way you do business. The amount you need to spend will depend entirely on you. If you are a self-starter and can get and stay fit on your own you probably won't need a personal trainer, but if you are like me and need to have someone stalking you to get you moving, you will have to allocate money to this.

I find it quite strange that we are so focused on having money when we retire yet we devote very little time or money to maintaining our health and wellbeing in the meantime to ensure we get there! From where I sit I don't want to ever retire, and I certainly don't plan to. But I do want to be healthy and full of energy until the day I die. Investing in my health and wellbeing today is far more important to me than my retirement fund. You may disagree, but as always it's up to the individual.

The moral to this tip is that to fuel the changes necessary to have a long, healthy and rewarding life in which business is a major component, it is very likely that you will have to be prepared to invest time, energy and money on a regular basis.

What can I do today?

How much time, energy and money are you prepared to invest in yourself to get your life the way you want it to be? Clearly this is not an easy question to answer, but it is a great question to ask. There is no right or wrong amount, but the important message is the realisation that you will need to invest in your Life Bank.

Action page—What I need to do to regain balance in my life

---

3 | The words that come out of your mouth are as important as those you hear

In this section I address the negative thoughts that we hold as true, often without even realising it, and how they are reinforced by and manifested in what we say and do.

Often we think of balance and harmony as being about sitting on a mountain and chanting. Sure, that would be great, but a lot of the time we don't have a mountain handy and we need something a little more convenient. Closer to earth, simply changing what we say and how we say it can have an incredible impact on our sense of wellbeing.

It's a recognised truth that if you say something often enough, even if it's utterly wrong, eventually you will come to believe it and so will the people around you. Here we examine some of the negative speech and thought patterns that lead to a sense of being overwhelmed and to a loss of balance—and, most importantly, what you can do about it.

#13   What are the limiting beliefs that keep your life out of control?
#14   Make a list of the negative words you use and burn it
#15   What words describe your life now and in the future?
#16   Avoid getting caught on *Steamship Misery*

#17   Gossiping, moaning and complaining—end it today!

#18   Identify the people who cause you problems and do something about them

#19   When you start to lose control—stop, breathe and regain focus

#20   Compliment others, be positive to others, be supportive of others

#13 What are the limiting beliefs that keep your life out of control?

Limiting beliefs are very interesting. Most of us have inherited them from our parents or other influential people in our lives, or even from the media. These can be beliefs that stop us from excelling in life.

I saw an extreme example of a limiting belief on a trip to Sri Lanka recently. In an elephant orphanage, the elephants seemed to be held in their places by a length of string tied around one back leg. Clearly the elephants could have broken away in a second but apparently they never did. The reason for this was explained by one of the handlers.

When the elephant babies are brought in to the centre a chain is attached to one leg to hold them in their pens. Of course they struggle and fight, but eventually they give up, accepting that whenever they are chained it is pointless to resist. Over time the chain is replaced by a thick rope, then a thinner and thinner rope until it is virtually little more than a piece of string. By now, however, the slightest pressure on the elephant's leg makes it think it cannot move from that particular spot. Without going into the ethics of this treatment, it is clear to see how a limiting belief is used to control the elephants.

People are not a lot different. We all have our own limiting beliefs. Many books have been written about this concept, and various ways developed to overcome our negative core beliefs.

In business I see the following five major negative beliefs every day. I believe they really do stop people from succeeding, and make life so much harder for business owners than it has to be:

1. Small business is meant to be hard.
2. You have to work really long hours to be successful in your own business.
3. You can never make huge amounts of money in a small business.

4. You have to sacrifice a lot to have your own business.
5. Most small businesses fail.

Now then—if you hold these core beliefs, why on earth are you in business? I have to admit, somewhat shamefacedly, that I held them myself for many years, and saw it almost as a personal challenge to prove them wrong.

Over time, and with the beneficial advice of too many people to list here, I came to realise these beliefs are *not right*.

- There is no reason at all why owning a small business should be tougher than any other way of making a living.
- Working really long hours is not a prerequisite to building a successful business.
- I know many, many people who have made and are making millions of dollars per year from their small business.
- I don't consider anything I do in business to be a sacrifice—it is more a matter of determining my priorities.
- Most small businesses fail for very predictable reasons. If you are aware of these pitfalls your chances of success are very high.

What negative beliefs are holding you back? Search deep within and see what nerves are touched when you explore some of the above thoughts. Once you have identified your limiting beliefs, replace each one with a positive belief. It takes time to change negative beliefs, but with perseverance you will.

What can I do today?

Identify your own negative beliefs, whatever they may be. Write each one down and then alongside it write a positive belief you want to have instead. From this point on, read the positive versions every day for at least a month.

#14 Make a list of the negative words you use and burn it

I got into a nasty habit a while back. Whenever friends, colleagues or associates asked how I was, my standard response would be something along the lines of: 'I'm so busy I can't do any more. It's ridiculous—I'm working really long hours, I'm not sure if I'm getting anywhere, and I'm certainly not looking for any more clients.' This response was a reaction to being very busy for a number of years.

Then things started to happen that made me realise I was heading down a dangerous road. One day I actually listened to what I was saying when a friend asked me how things were going; to my shock I realised I'd responded with my standard tirade without even stopping to think how things really were going. My friend's eyes glazed over, my mouth was on automatic pilot. As this weird, negative little action went on, I realised I was reinforcing my negative beliefs.

The second notable thing was that people stopped referring clients to me. I noticed that my referral rate was dropping and at first I thought that maybe I was doing something wrong—well, I was, but it wasn't what I thought. I asked a few close colleagues why, expecting to hear some bad news. They looked at me, quite surprised, and said, 'Andrew, you are always so busy. We didn't want to send you any more clients because you made it clear you didn't want any more.'

What a realisation! I had to rebuild my entire thought and speech process, to retrain myself. I made a list of the words, phrases, terms and quotes I used that were negative—and there were quite a few. I made a commitment to myself to stop using them from that day on, and I did. In fact, as soon as I started to use a 'standard response' of any kind I would stop talking, collect my thoughts and begin again. Eventually I didn't need my list anymore, so I took it off the wall and burned it.

I suggest you do the same. If we tell people often enough that life is horrible, it's so hard to run your own business, staff are terrible, the market is down, we are doing it tough financially, we materialise these thoughts into reality.

If you turn these negatives into positives, the results are astounding. My rate of referrals has since gone through the roof and I will never ever moan about how busy I am again.

What can I do today?

Make up a list of the negative terms, words, phrases and quotes that are limiting you. Make a conscious effort to eliminate them from your life and replace them with positive, energetic and enthusiastic responses. When you are ready, burn the list of the old limiting words—you will never need them again.

#15 What words describe your life now and in the future?

Make a list of the words that describe your life now and how you would like it to be in the future. This tip follows on from the last, but it is a little more specific about how you can change the way you think. In my experience, the people who are positive and energetic about their life and their business are always much happier and more balanced. If you listen closely to what they say you will see that their words reflect their thoughts—and that is the key.

Recently I was having a massage to relieve pain from holding too much stress in my neck. The masseuse talked and talked, which was beginning to drive me crazy because I was in so much pain. But then I decided to stop feeling sorry for myself and started listening to her. She was amazing. She was raving about how much she loved her job—being able to meet people, look out the window into her garden, travel from place to place. I thought she must have been new to the game, but she then went on to say she had been doing it for 20 years. I was dumbfounded. Twenty years of rubbing oil on strangers' backs and she loved it as much today as the day she started. Extraordinary.

All too often we find it a struggle to identify what it is we like about our lives and what we don't like. I made up an exercise for myself a few years ago in which I started with a description of how I saw my life at the time—what I liked, what I didn't like and what I wanted to change. Then I wrote another description about how I wanted my life to be, right down to how much money I wanted to earn, what type of woman I wanted to be in a relationship with, where I wanted to travel to and when, and even what kind of car I wanted to drive.

So here I had two bits of paper, one in each hand. One said where I was today and the other described where I wanted to be. Now I could get a clear picture in my head of where I was heading and why.

This is a very powerful exercise on many levels. For starters, it makes you stop and think about what is missing in your life and what you really want to achieve. Statistically, less than 5 per cent of people have written goals like this. Interestingly enough, the people who are the most successful normally fit into that group.

Defining the goals that you want to achieve can be tough. I tend to break them up into a few categories, including business, relationship, health, financial and spiritual. Regardless of how you want to go about defining where you are going, just doing it is a great start. Be a little flexible. It isn't an exam with right or wrong answers.

What can I do today?

Write down all the things about your life that you like or don't like on a piece of paper. Then, on a separate piece of paper, write down how you would like your life to be. Make it as specific as you can.

#16 Avoid getting caught on *Steamship Misery*

I talk to a lot of small business owners around the world. Interestingly, no matter which country I'm in, there seems to be a common misconception that small business is supposed to be tough, otherwise you aren't doing it right. I call this 'Small Business Syndrome', and I believe it really holds small business owners back.

Small Business Syndrome relates to all the negatives of having a small business—and yes, there are a number of them, but in my opinion the positives far outweigh the negatives. And let's be honest: if they didn't, why on earth would you ever start your own business?

Anyone who has been in small business for any period of time will have heard all the lines about how hard it is. Staff are nothing but trouble, suppliers always let you down, money is always tight, the hours you have to work are crazy, the stress you have to endure will ultimately break you, and so on. This suffering is normally passed on in self-pity workshops with other small business owners (and I will talk about these workshops a little later).

I love my business. I describe it as exciting, energetic and stimulating. I can come and go as I please, I get to make decisions on the spot about how business is done, if I work hard I earn more, I contribute to society through my business and get to build relationships with incredible people, many of whom work with me. Sure, I have all the other stuff to deal with as well, but I don't focus on that anywhere near as much as I focus on the good stuff.

It's easy to forget the good points about having your own business. The grass is always greener elsewhere, and we think that everyone else's business is better than ours. Well, I have a surprise for you—it's not true! Common misconception: how hard can it be to run a restaurant? Cook a few meals, serve them up and the customers keep rolling in. I don't think so.

Ask anyone who has owned their own restaurant and you will hear a very specific tale about running a tough business.

Every single business has good points and bad points. The difference is which points you decide to focus on.

What can I do today?

Think about all the positive aspects of your business. Write them down. Whenever you find yourself feeling a little blue or depressed about what you are doing, read through the list to remind yourself just how good it really is.

#17 Gossiping, moaning and complaining—end it today!

When you are feeling overwhelmed, out of control, depressed or negative, your conversation tends to be less than positive. This is when gossiping, moaning and complaining slip into the conversation. Unfortunately, after a while they become the norm.

I have a client I meet with once a week. He spends the first half-hour of our meeting moaning and complaining about the company he works for. It is tragic and sad and, to be honest, very depressing. My advice to him is always the same—leave. Find a company where you will be happy; life is far too short for ongoing misery.

There is absolutely nothing to be gained from gossiping, moaning and complaining; on the contrary, it has a long-term negative effect on those around you. It can also start to create a corporate culture that revolves around this mentality. Gossip only works if it is passed on.

Creating a positive, nurturing environment is far more important and the rewards are far greater. But it takes an effort to break the cycle if it already exists in your business—and you may be the main culprit.

Every time you find yourself starting to gossip, moan or complain, stop yourself in your tracks and rethink what you were going to say. If you have staff gossiping, moaning or complaining to you, let them know that you are simply not interested. Tell them that you don't like to gossip, moan or complain—you have moved on. Some people won't like this, but tough. (With reference to the client I was talking about, sometimes it's not so easy to put a stop to it. It may be that the only answer is to drop such clients if they are too depressing.)

Balance and harmony in life is as much about what you say and hear as it is about what you see and do. Negativity breeds negativity; positivity breeds success.

What can I do today?

Make a concerted effort from this minute on not to get involved in gossiping, moaning or complaining, in any shape or form.

#18 Identify the people who cause you problems and do something about them

Just as we develop negative thought patterns that are reinforced by negative language, there are often people in our lives who further reinforce these beliefs and literally bring us down by what they say and do.

We all have friends who make us wince when they walk in. We know that within five minutes they will have us completely depressed, and feeling that there is nothing we can do about it. Their lives are desperate, sad, tragic, bored or whatever, and odds on you have a sympathetic ear, so you listen and they keep coming back to tell you more.

Do you know why? Because it makes them feel better. They make you feel like you want to jump out the nearest window, and they leave whistling and smelling the roses. Now this is crazy.

If you are surrounded by people like this, it's not going to be hard to change—it's going to be near impossible. It may be hard to get them out of your life because they're your biggest customer, a relative or your business partner. But whatever else you do, you really do need to draw a line in the sand. If more of the people you mix with are negative than positive, you have a problem, which will only get worse over time and keep you trapped in the cycle of feeling overwhelmed.

I made a very conscious decision a number of years ago about the type of people I would have in my life. I want to be surrounded by energetic, enthusiastic and positive people who are getting on with their lives. I don't care what they do for a living, how much money they have or who they know. All I care about is their zest for life. These people inspire me and motivate me to be the best person I can be; they are supportive of any decision or change that will help me to achieve this goal. If I fail, they are the first people to support me and say at least I gave it a go.

If I listened to the negative people I wouldn't do anything, because life is clearly so damn messed up that there is nothing I can possibly do that would make it any better. There is no malicious intent in these people, it's just a reflection of where they are at in life at the time. And that is sad, but we all need to decide if we want to be equally sad. I made the decision not to and that was that.

I suggest that you develop a way of keeping such people at arm's length. Some of them won't like you for it, and they will tell you so. Be prepared for some repercussions, but stay resilient because the pay-off is big. If you don't know where to find positive, energetic, enthusiastic people, ask around. They are normally busy people who are getting on with life. The people sitting around in coffee shops and bars all day long clearly have too much time on their hands.

What can I do today?

Identify the people around you who fit in the negative category and start making a plan of how you will get them out of your life, or at least minimise the impact they have on you. At the same time, make a list of the places where you might be able to meet and mix with positive, like-minded people.

#19 When you start to lose control—stop, breathe and regain focus

Being overwhelmed and feeling out of control in your business is a terrible feeling. Sometimes you just don't know where to turn. There are hundreds of emails that need answering, a pile of telephone messages to return, correspondence to read, meetings to be had, deadlines of every kind, staff needing direction—and then you get the call saying there is a problem with your biggest customer, and it's a doozy.

If all this sounds like your normal kind of day—and it's only 9 a.m.—no wonder you are feeling a little out of control and in need of some balance and harmony in your life. I can relate completely. When you are in the midst of an over-whelming downer, it's easy to slide even lower. Taking a moment to rethink and regroup is the best thing you can possibly do here.

A friend of mine who is a pilot said that this is one of the key training techniques used in flight school. When things are starting to go pear-shaped, simply take a moment to stop every-thing, take a big, deep breath and think logically about what you are doing. Sounds simple, doesn't it, but we rarely do it.

A good friend of mine who has had the pleasure of watching me over the years going from periods of Zen monk calmness to sheer madness gave me a sticker that simply said 'JUST BREATHE'. And it is advice I will take to the grave.

Years ago I had problems with anxiety attacks. I was a commercial diver at the time so, as you can imagine, it's not good to experience a panic attack 50 metres below the surface. The psychologist said a similar thing at the time: 'You have to learn to breathe.' At the time I was not very impressed by these words of wisdom, thinking I had clearly just wasted hundreds of dollars seeing a crazy woman, but as the years went by and I did learn to breathe, I realised just how right she was.

When we are stressed and freaked out we breathe very shallowly. This makes us feel short of breath and even more stressed, which of course stresses us out even further. It's a nasty cycle.

If you can learn to stop, take a few very deep breaths and then do what you need to do, the results will be far better and your feelings of being out of control will be greatly reduced in intensity. It is simply a matter of reprogramming your normal response mechanism, which is to dive in and try to fix everything at once.

What can I do today?

Learn to breathe. Put a big sign on the wall: 'JUST BREATHE'. And the very next time you are feeling the pangs of being 'out of control' starting to surface, stop, take a few deep breaths and then act. It will take a while to reprogram yourself, but when you've done it, life will become much easier.

#20 Compliment others, be positive to others, be supportive of others

One of the greatest books I have ever read in my life is *How to Win Friends and Influence People* by that master of people interaction, Dale Carnegie. This book has been my bible for almost 20 years and I make a point of reading it again every year, at least once. I am sure this sounds a little crazy, but let me explain.

This book was written over 70 years ago, in 1936. It shows you, in very simple terms, how to get the best out of people. The concepts Carnegie raises are as relevant now as they were then. His underlying theme focuses on the power of being genuinely positive and encouraging of the people we deal with on a daily basis.

The book shows the importance of being supportive of others, of listening and being interested in people. The most amazing and truly wonderful aspect of this is that the more you support others, the more you listen, the more interested and encouraging of other people you are, the more these same characteristics flow back to you in your daily life. While that should never be your reason for offering support and encouragement, it is a beautiful reward.

Something as simple as offering a compliment to the person serving you in the grocery store on the way to work can change their entire outlook for the day, and yours as well. The best time to be like this is when you are feeling the most out of control or out of balance. Take your focus off yourself and put it onto others.

Have you ever noticed how, when you are in your own world and someone compliments you, perhaps saying how nice your shirt is, for instance, you are forced to take a step back and stop for a moment to take the compliment in? It certainly makes you feel warm inside, doesn't it?

I try to be positive and complimentary to every single person I meet. Sometimes that is pretty hard, in fact it can be downright impossible at times, because some people are just too angry to even register a compliment. But in return, my life is filled with people being incredibly supportive, loving and nurturing to me, especially when I need it the most.

What can I do today?

Next time you are feeling really stressed out start dishing out the compliments. Make them sincere, because there is nothing worse than shallow, insincere compliments—they don't fool anyone. And if you haven't already got a copy, go out today and buy Dale Carnegie's classic, *How to Win Friends and Influence People.*

Action page—What I need to do to regain balance in my life

----

4 | The 'F' factor—bring it on

There is no doubt that if you are having fun in whatever it is you do, the feeling of being overwhelmed, out of control or out of balance simply can't take hold—at the bare minimum, its effects will be lessened. For many people the loss of joy they experience on a daily basis is the most confronting aspect of leading a life that is out of harmony. As we say throughout this book, having a full and demanding life is not necessarily a bad thing—but having a life without laughter most certainly is.

I know that for many people the whole concept of having fun at work is a little 'odd', something that's hard to come to grips with. You may consider it somewhat 'out there', or perhaps not a real business issue. Well, without going into the reams of research that support the idea, we *need* to spend a lot more time having fun in our day-to-day lives, especially at work, simply because it makes life so much more enjoyable and so much less stressful and out of control.

This section looks at ways to bring the 'F' factor back into your life, and to me it is the most important information you will find in this book.

#21   Do you remember when you used to laugh a lot?
#22   Professionalism vs fun
#23   Surround yourself with the things that make you warm inside

#21 Do you remember when you used to laugh a lot?

Day-to-day pressure builds up over time. One of its most noticeable symptoms is that the amount of laughter in a person's life tends to drop proportionally as pressure and stress increase. Why we stop laughing is really unclear, but the weight of the world on our shoulders is a heavy burden regardless of where we are in life. The pressures of day-to-day living are as relevant to the high school teenager facing exams as they are to the head of a corporation with 100 000 employees.

We all look sympathetic when the 'pressure' of running a large corporation makes the CEO miserable, yet we say that teenagers are being melodramatic when impending exams make them lose their sense of humour. I have to reinforce the fact that all pressure is relevant and important to the person feeling it. There are no universal measures saying that the feelings one person experiences are more important or significant than any other person's.

One thing is certain, though: most of us remember times when we had less pressure and stress in our lives, fewer demands on our time, our money and our energy, and generally these were times when we were quick to laugh and quick to make others laugh. We rolled with the punches, we took setbacks in our stride and we didn't seem to take life quite so seriously. Well, you can have those times back again, and this book is intended to help you find them.

Take a moment to think back to that time in your life when you used to laugh the most. Close your eyes and spend a few minutes with this visualisation. Start to think about that time when you felt so carefree and happy. What year was it? What was happening in your life? Where were you living? Who were you spending time with? Where did you work? What were you wearing? What did you do on weekends? What music were you listening to? What were you reading? What kind of car did you drive? Where did you hang out? What smells remind you of that time?

Now open your eyes and spend a few moments jotting down the words that best describe your emotions and feelings when you think about that time. What was it that made your life feel so good? I am sure that even then there was a lot of pressure—money could have been an issue, relationships might have come and gone, a lack of certainty about the future might have figured highly, among other challenges. Even so, the feelings you remember most are joy and happiness and being carefree. So what is the difference between then and now?

Identifying this difference is a significant point. Try to find the one word that describes what has changed for you. Because once you know this word, you know your enemy and you can finally do something about it.

As an example, let's say that the one word affecting you is 'pressure', meaning that you feel so much more pressure to perform, to deliver, to provide—whatever. Now you have a name for what has to change in your life. While it won't be that easy to remove the pressure, it is relatively easy to change the way you perceive it, react to it and think about it.

Doing this exercise on a regular basis, when you're feeling overwhelmed and anxious, will have a very positive effect. It will help you to change your life and the way you deal with the main issues preventing you from achieving balance.

What can I do today?

Do the visualisation described above. It will make you feel good, it will bring a smile to your face, it will reduce the feeling of being overwhelmed that we all experience at times. Best of all, it will remind you what it's like to feel that sensation of joy again.

#22 Professionalism vs fun

Being considered professional is a goal that the vast majority of business owners strive for, and rightly so. Our customers expect professionalism, and when a business doesn't deliver, look out. But what exactly is professionalism and what does it mean to be professional?

The reason I ask these questions is that I believe many business owners don't allow fun into their workplace because they feel it's unprofessional and their customers won't like it or that it will somehow diminish their perceptions of the business.

I completely disagree with this notion, and say right here and now that one of the most effective ways to build a dynamic and successful business is to have a workplace that actively encourages people to have a good time. And by people, I mean staff, customers, suppliers, cleaners—whoever has some kind of interaction with this business.

Think back to the last time you visited a business where it seemed like everyone was having a good time. Did you think that what they delivered was any less professional because they were joking around, laughing or enjoying themselves? I doubt it. If you haven't read the book *Fish! Tales: Real-Life Stories to Help You Transform Your Workplace and Your Life*, grab it today. It begins with an amazing story about a retail fishmonger business in Seattle, on the West Coast of the United States, that has become internationally renowned for its philosophy of building a successful business through an energetic, dynamic, fun-filled workplace.

I know of a legal firm that plays lawyer jokes on their on-hold telephone system. These legal eagles are very successful. Their clients love them, they deliver exceptional service and they get results. Their advertising is fun and they enjoy laughing at themselves and the legal profession as a whole. Does this make them less professional? Not in my eyes, certainly not in the eyes of their clients, and I would hazard a guess and say not in the eyes of their bank manager either.

Surely customers would much rather be in an environment where the people they are doing business with are having a good time? Where everyone is quick to smile, light-hearted and clearly in a good mood? Surely staff would want to work for a company that has a reputation as a place where people enjoy going to work?

The important point here is to develop your own philosophy around professionalism vs fun. Clearly define both as they apply to your business. What are your goals and objectives when it comes to being considered professional? How do you want to be perceived by your customers? What is your philosophy about having fun at work? What are the boundaries when it comes to having fun? After all, you aren't running a circus. Why not develop a 'having fun and being professional' philosophy that clearly defines how you see the relationship between professionalism and fun, what you see as positive and to be encouraged and what should be avoided.

Welcome fun back into your working life; encourage it, enjoy it, spread it around, but define the boundaries so that everyone knows what is OK and what is not. Try it in little steps first and start to notice how your customers respond. I have no doubt that you will be pleasantly surprised by their reaction.

What can I do today?

Develop your own 'having fun and being professional' philosophy. Once you have perceptions of both concepts clear in your own mind, they will reach a balance in your workplace if you let them. Make sure you share this philosophy with those around you.

#23 Surround yourself with the things that make you warm inside

Let me describe my office. I have a big antique desk that was once the stationmaster's desk at a little country train station. It's made from silky oak, a magnificent light-coloured timber. I have a large whiteboard with my current projects listed on it, and some philosophical and motivational messages. I have a picture board behind my desk with hundreds of photos of people from around the world that I have collected over the years. I have an abstract picture of Venice painted by a very close friend, as well as countless books and magazines, work-related and otherwise. A good stereo and an excellent collection of CDs to while away those late working nights (and, of course, I have now embraced the world of iPod). I also have wood carvings from a brief stint in Papua New Guinea, gifts from clients, copies of my previous books published in different languages, vitamin tablets, a change of clothes—and much more.

My office reflects my life—it is full, sometimes organised, often chaotic, but always rich, colourful and interesting. I have the philosophy that if I am going to spend a lot of time in my office—and I do—I want to feel at home there, comfortable and relaxed. Having all these things in my office makes me feel that way, and no matter how stressed I may feel or how over-whelmed I am, I always breathe a sigh of relief when I sit down at my desk.

I am a firm believer in the importance of feeling as though you are part of the area where you work. Sometimes a photo of the family in a 6 × 4 frame on the desk just isn't enough. You might think it is—but if you feel like a visitor to your workspace rather than a part of it, maybe you need to create more of a connection. Again, as a business owner, I think that we should encourage our staff to do the same. Clearly there are boundaries (imagine a king-size bed in the accountant's office), but you can easily define these and, just as I discussed in tip #22, about embracing a little fun in the workplace, bringing personality into a business is not unprofessional in the slightest.

The calming effect of having a few of your favourite things with you at work can be quite amazing. If you aren't convinced, give it a go anyway and see if it makes a difference to you.

What can I do today?

What changes can you make to your workplace that will make it more enjoyable or pleasant? Maybe it's time to look with new eyes at where you work, and once and for all make it appeal to you as a place where you feel safe and comfortable. Often the way to go about it is to remove the clutter, have a good clean-up and simply start again. Is there something irritating about your workplace that adds to your day-to-day stress? Can you stop everything and change that one thing? You might be surprised at the difference this can make to your day-to-day life.

#24 The boomerang effect of being light-hearted

It's interesting to see how quickly a smile is returned, a light-hearted comment acknowledged or a laugh answered with a laugh. Remembering to let ourselves be light-hearted is important in the process of overcoming any out-of-balance state we might find ourselves in.

I take what I do seriously. I am a hard taskmaster because I set high standards for myself and for those around me, borne of a very real desire to be exceptional at what I do. But as I constantly remind everyone who works with me, at the end of the day it is only business, and we should never lose sight of this. In the scale of things, sure, our businesses are pretty darn important, but they are nowhere near as important as our health or our relationships with our family.

So if we keep business in perspective, we can take the time to smile, to laugh and to be a little light-hearted. And the best part is that the more you do this the more other people will treat you the same way. Spread it around, give compliments, have a laugh at yourself when things go wrong. Remember not to take yourself too seriously—after all, it is only business.

What can I do today?

Put a big sign up on your wall: 'It is only business.' Then go out and spread the fun gene, encourage people to be a little playful, read a joke book, have a laugh at yourself and generally lighten up. Notice how this gets boomeranged back to you and, most importantly, how much better you start to feel as the humour mill starts to turn.

#25 Political correctness in the world of fun

This is the only real word of warning in this section and it would be remiss of me not to spell out some of the boundaries we need to take into consideration when it comes to embracing fun in the workplace. Unfortunately, there is nearly always someone who oversteps the mark, so that what is meant as good-spirited humour can sometimes cause offence and very genuine distress to another member of the team.

Many businesses live in fear of litigation and tend to have a blanket approach that ends up meaning no jokes about anything. I think there is a middle road that can be followed without taking the soul out of a business. The most important part of this equation is to make clear to any new members of staff what your policy or views are regarding what can be said and what can't be said to other members of staff.

Some small businesses tend to have pretty liberal views on forwarding internet jokes, while others are seriously draconian about it. You need to decide what your policy is; if you are not sure about it ask your industry association, business mentors or professional advisors for an opinion. Then be clear on what your policy is and make sure everyone else is clear as well.

I make a point of asking any of my new staff members if they have any personal issues that could lead to their being seriously offended, and if there is a point that needs to be discussed it is raised with the other staff members in an appropriate manner. This way we can all still get a laugh from email jokes, but we are sensitive when we need to be. The responsibility is shared and rather than me being the watchdog we all act in a mature and responsible manner.

So in short, be politically correct but not soulless. Don't lose the fun and energy of your business through a fear-based decision on political correctness or litigation.

THE 'F' FACTOR—BRING IT ON

What can I do today?

Determine your company view on the boundaries that you feel are appropriate (and legal) when it comes to having fun at work, and make sure you put it in writing. Then give it to your staff. Remember the philosophy that, if in doubt, avoid race, religion, sex and politics (but then often there isn't a lot left to laugh about!).

#26 Creating 'magnificent moments' every single day

Every day we are presented with an incredible array of opportunities, and when you own your own business you are often faced with more than your share. These opportunities take many shapes and forms but, sadly, when we are feeling out of control we rarely see them because we are too busy looking inwards, muttering under our breath and feeling sorry for ourselves.

One way to really overcome this feeling is to stop focusing on your woes, on yourself, and spend a few moments focusing on someone else. It is incredibly therapeutic for both you and the other person. The aim here is to create a few 'magnificent moments' every single day we are on the planet.

So, I hear you ask, what are these 'magnificent moments'? Well, they are simple interactions where you make the effort to make someone else's day bolder, brighter and more colourful. I call it a conscious interaction, one where you are in the moment, not just going through the motions.

'Magnificent moments' (also known as 'random acts of kindness') can happen at any time, day or night. They can be as simple as striking up a conversation with someone you see every day but never actually talk to. Perhaps the person behind the counter at your local shop or the petrol station where you fill your car. Introduce yourself, tell them what you do, and thank them for doing what they do to make your day a little easier.

What other opportunities are there to create these conscious interactions? There are so many I could write a book about it. You could send me an email, for instance, to say how much you like this book, or send a thankyou card to a client, make a donation to a charity on someone else's behalf, visit a rest home and get to know a few of the residents, give a member of your team an early mark, pay the toll for the car behind you or put some money in a parking meter that is set to run out.

'Magnificent moments' are exactly that—moments. You don't want to spend an hour with the person, or stalk them or freak them out. Simply break the normal interactions of their day and show some genuine interest in them.

I try to create as many of these conscious interactions as I can every day. To be honest, I sometimes feel a little selfish doing it because the energy I get back and the feelings of warmth, affection and appreciation at times seem far greater than what I give.

To bring your life back into balance, take some of the focus off you and find out about those around you. Make their day a little special and yours will be, too.

What can I do today?

Like any new skill, creating 'magnificent moments' might take a little practice. Why not make the decision to create one 'magnificent moment' every day for the next week? You might grow to like it so much that it becomes a habit. I certainly hope so.

#27 Remember to stop, think and laugh

Often when we get caught up in mayhem, we lose our tempers and our sense of humour. I found myself in this situation many times in the past. And, what was worse, I tended to overreact to situations that really didn't warrant it. Then, of course, you know that you have overreacted and try to fix the damage—but it's awkward.

I learned a good lesson from several close friends who ran very busy and full-on businesses that were far more demanding than mine. I was amazed at the way they would receive bad news about an unhappy customer or a lost shipment or some other unfortunate incident—things that would have made me rant and rave for an hour. They would stop, think for a moment, make a joke and then deal with it. They didn't get emotional or overreact, but they did think about the situation, conduct a quick mental evaluation, and then lighten the mood and move on to deal with the problem.

This is a characteristic I have noticed in many excellent leaders—their ability to deal with a situation in a cool, calm manner and not lose their sense of humour.

Earlier in the book I mentioned that the key to change was to take some time to stop and think situations through rather than immediately react. We need to stop, think and then act. Normally things are not as bad as they first appear, but in an overwhelmed, stressed-out state we tend to take everything a little more personally than we normally would. It is part of the cycle. So we get angry easily, we get short with people and we tend to put on the martyr hat. (How could they do this to me? To get anything done right around here I have to do it myself.)

What can I do today?

Think back over the past week. Were there any situations you feel you could have handled better if you had taken some time to stop, think and laugh? Challenge yourself to rise to the occasion the very next time you are faced with a situation that would normally make you lose it. Find some humour in the situation and deal with it. You will become a better leader, your staff will learn from you and respect you and, most importantly, a load will be lifted from your shoulders.

#28 The myth of time-wasting (the six-minute increment)

Sometimes it is time well spent simply to stop and have a chat and some social interaction. It builds bonds, reduces stress and encourages people to feel that they are part of a team.

The days of the business 'overlord' are long gone; progressive businesses are looking for ways to encourage their staff to be productive in their own way. At long last we realise that people work in different ways. Trying to squeeze everyone into the same mould is an outdated concept.

The reference in the heading to the six-minute increment relates to the common practice in professional services firms, like accounting and law firms, for staff to have to report on how their time was spent (and which client should be billed) for every six-minute period. Clearly a good way to encourage productivity and accountability, but it does create a stressful environment and isn't overly conducive to free-thinking, creativity and individuality—traits once considered a problem but now highly sought after.

There is no doubt that some people do waste time and probably don't do their job as effectively as they should. But there needs to be some understanding that as human beings we are social animals, which means we need time to interact and be social. Sure, there are breaks for this, but as business owners, the better our staff perform the greater the results we achieve. If they are happy and surrounded by a positive environment that is enjoyable to work in, they will do better work—trust in the system.

What can I do today?

Start to reprogram the way you think. Don't make your staff feel uncomfortable when you come around. Get to know them better and look at this time as a significant investment in the future of your business. It is amazing what you can learn about your business when you take the time to talk to those who actually run it.

#29 Fun uses every sense—sight, sound, touch, smell and taste

The aim of this section is to introduce a little fun into your business, to lighten it up and help restore a sense of balance, enjoyment and fulfilment at work. Fun, in whatever form it takes, has an amazingly restorative ability. Humour is a very potent weapon in the small business skills arsenal.

Unfortunately, terminal seriousness has crept into many workplaces, and many business owners wanting to lighten up the place a little don't know where to start. So I have made it easy for you. Here are ten good ways to encourage your team to laugh a little more often; hopefully you will, too!

1. Develop a Fun Committee—this committee's job is to come up with ideas for making your workplace a whole lot more fun. (People need to volunteer for this, and ideally need a good sense of humour.)
2. Joke of the day—share the responsibility around and get everyone to take turns at coming up with a joke of the day.
3. Ugly shirt day—while many businesses already look as if they are holding this competition every day, make it a special event.
4. Baby pictures—have a pin-up board with baby pictures of every member of your team—and you!
5. Have a fun zone—this can be where people go when they need to laugh. It can have a few silly toys, some joke books—really, anything that can raise a smile.
6. Baking day—have a rotating roster for everyone to bake something and bring it into work. There must be guidelines to make it equal and everyone should at least try the end result.
7. Have a weekly buddy system—everyone gets allocated a buddy for one week, and the buddy has to look after the

'boss', get them tea and coffee, buy their lunch, and so on. But the catch is, the next week, you swap.

8. Introduce spontaneity—take your team out for coffee, bring in a treat or just do something out of the ordinary.
9. Successes Board of Fame—have a noticeboard with staff successes for the month. This can be any success, not just work related.
10. Have a 'something you didn't know about me' day—every member of your team tells the rest of the team one thing that no one at work would know about them.

What can I do today?

Start having more fun at work today. If your workplace is a little humour-challenged, give it time, don't try to turn it into the local comedy club overnight. Start small, work your way up, but start today. And remember that laughing is also an excellent form of rejuvenation—15 minutes of laughter has the same relaxing effect as meditating for eight hours; ten minutes of laughter has the same relaxing effect as two hours' sleep.

#30 As the boss, you are the business barometer

As the boss, the business owner, the manager, the partner—whatever position you hold, there is no doubt that the person at the top sets the mood for the culture within an organisation.

Whether you are uptight, stressed out, serious, angry or bored, this feeling will be reflected in those around you. If you don't care about the business, how can you expect your staff to? For this reason alone, the wellbeing of your business is intrinsically linked to your wellbeing, and your state of mind is a critical component in this process.

One interesting observation I have made on the health and wellbeing of a business is that if the person at the top smokes, for instance, there will generally be more smokers in the business. If the person at the top drinks a lot, there will be more heavy drinkers in the business. I don't know whether this is a case of like attracting like or whether certain trends are simply characteristic of certain industries, but it is an effect I have seen in many businesses. And it works the same way on an attitude level—a business run by someone who is miserable tends to attract miserable staff (and often miserable customers, too).

Of course, the best part of this effect is that it tends to work equally well in the positive. Businesses run by a person with self-respect, a positive and energetic attitude, and a 'can do' philosophy tend to attract staff with the same outlook on life. People who like to have fun at work attract other people who like to have fun at work. What an amazing opportunity this represents.

The key message here is to understand that if you are the top of your immediate food chain, it is important that you have a positive, energetic attitude to life and business so that you can attract like-minded people and set the culture for your business. These like-minded people will in turn make your business more successful, and your life will get easier and the day-to-day pressures you feel will be reduced.

THE 'F' FACTOR—BRING IT ON

What can I do today?

On your way to work take a moment to focus on your view of the day ahead. What message do you want to give to your staff and customers, remembering that they will be a reflection of you? Visualise how your interactions will look and feel, then make them a reality.

Action page—What I need to do to regain balance in my life

----

5 | Beware the energy drain

The battle for balance is really an energy issue. As business owners try to juggle work and home, the competing demands of each slowly erode overall energy levels. From a state of depleted energy, everything gets just that little bit harder. This forms a vicious cycle, where everyday challenges can seem insurmountable, and you stop being able to make decisions and start to suffer from stress-related health problems.

As this is happening, your energy keeps draining away and the simplest of problems can ultimately trigger a disproportionately monumental breakdown.

This section looks at some of the main reasons for the emotional energy drain and provides some simple advice to overcome it.

#31   Learn to let go
#32   Master the art of saying no
#33   Separate work from home—relationship issues
#34   If you lie down with dogs you get up with fleas
#35   Managing money issues
#36   Don't be afraid to sack some customers
#37   The torture of perfection
#38   Do the work you love—give the rest to others
#39   The more you give the more you get back
#40   Take off the medals—it shouldn't be that hard

#31 Learn to let go

I have a friend who was always successful in business and became very wealthy. Then, through a series of misfortunes, his business failed and he went broke. He has never got over it. Although at the time of his business failure he was quite young and easily had the ability, the resourcefulness and the ideas to start again, he turned into a bitter and angry man who blamed the world for his loss.

Holding on to past failures and mistakes takes a lot of energy. One of the best lessons I have learned, not only in business but also in life, has been the art of letting go.

It's hard to find a new lover if you are eaten up with anger and resentment towards the ex who broke your heart. You might not even realise that you are still holding the flame. How can you build a successful business, then, if you are still bitter and twisted about losing the last one? You struggle on day after day, trying to make it work and wondering why it doesn't, and all the while this very struggle to succeed reinforces and perpetuates the bitterness.

A long time ago I had a business partner who took literally everything I owned. He left me with a pile of debts and a battered and bruised ego. I spent many years feeling really angry with him, thinking about how to get revenge. Then one morning I woke up and realised how much energy it was taking to hold on to this anger so tightly. I was physically suffering from my rage—I had boils all over my body, I wasn't sleeping, I was short-tempered and unhappy. That morning I decided to just let it all go, to learn from the situation, and to put a little faith in the universe and the law of karma. The change was amazing—my boils cleared up within a few days, I started to sleep like a baby and my whole disposition lightened so I could enjoy life again.

It's easy to find reasons to be bitter and twisted; I know I have plenty. My parents abandoned my sister and me when we were infants. It would have been easy to harbour anger towards them but I learned to understand why they did it, to empathise with a young couple—no more than kids themselves—who found themselves in a bad relationship. They did what they thought was best at the time—they left us with someone more able to look after us. If they hadn't done so, would I have gone on to become a bestselling author, successful entrepreneur and leader in my community? Somehow, I doubt it. So I am actually grateful that my parents left us.

The realisation that my parents' actions had enabled me to succeed was life-changing. Instead of struggling with feelings of resentment and abandonment I could simply be grateful. But this required me to look long and hard at the issue and think about it from a very different point of view, and then to simply get over it.

Identifying the issues you are holding on to that are draining you of energy is the first step to letting them go. Then you have to ask yourself two questions. First, what have you got to gain by holding on to this issue? And what have you got to gain by letting it go? For example, if you have been hurt in a previous relationship you can choose to hold back and never get close to anyone again. The upside is that you won't get hurt. The downside is that you will be really lonely, living a shallow and joyless life without the highs and lows of a close and intimate relationship.

Or, in a business context, if a member of your staff steals from you, it's easy to decide that you will never trust another employee. Worse still, you might start to imagine that everyone is trying to steal from you. You will become paranoid and spend all of your energy worrying about this issue. But how can you grow your business if you don't empower people and trust them to do the right thing?

Learning how to let go is a valuable lesson in life. It takes so much energy to hold on to negative issues.

What can I do today?

Have you got one issue in your business or personal life that you are not letting go of when, deep down, you really know you should? Today, look at the situation from a different perspective, and let it go once and for all.

#32 Master the art of saying no

Being responsible for everyone and everything is exhausting. Business owners often assume responsibility way beyond the call of duty, and this can become extremely stressful. A comment that I hear frequently from business owners is that they are tired of being responsible for everything to do with the business.

At the end of the day, however, you *are* responsible for everything to do with your business, but it is up to you how you interpret this responsibility. In fact, you need to share the responsibility around and empower others to take some of it from your shoulders.

This can be a little tricky at first, especially for the business owner who has developed the habit of saying yes to everything. Many of the tips in this book discuss ways to share the load, but the most powerful tool to ease the energy drain associated with responsibility overload is learning to say no. Let me show you how I did it.

I do a lot of public speaking and have a relatively high profile in my home city. The problem with this is that I am frequently asked to do free speaking jobs for charities and other organisations like universities and business groups. Often when I am asked I am put on the spot. In the past I didn't feel that I could say no. Then it felt like an extra commitment that really stressed me out and added to my already considerable workload. I always used to kick myself after I'd agreed to one of these engagements, but I didn't know how to stop this from happening.

Now I have a system that works fantastically for me. Whenever someone asks me to speak to their organisation, whether they ask me face to face, over the phone or by email, I never commit to an engagement on the spot. I always say that I have to check my diary and other commitments first and that it might take me a day or two to get back to them. This gives

71

me a little breathing space to decide if it is something I can do and, more importantly, something I want to do. If the answer to either of these is no, I call the person back and tell them that I can't do the event.

I can't overstate how much pressure this has taken off me. I follow this system with virtually every request for my time in my business life. You can also develop similar habits and buffers that simply give you room to properly consider a request on your time.

Learning to say no will certainly have a major impact on the day-to-day responsibilities and demands that so often cause undue stress and prevent any form of balance in our lives. Master the art of saying no and your life will change.

What can I do today?

Buy the book *How to Say No Without Feeling Guilty* by Patti Breitman and Connie Hatch. This book will certainly help you to overcome the impulse to say yes. In addition, work out your own system that will work for you so that you can start to say no more often.

#33 Separate work from home—relationship issues

Sometimes your business isn't the culprit for the lack of balance in your life. There is nothing more draining than the emotional confrontations that occur when you have relationship issues. Splitting up with a partner is considered by many to be the most stressful situation you will experience, apart from terminal illness. This is multiplied tenfold if you and your partner work together in your business.

I experienced this first hand: I started a business with my then wife, and later we went through a separation and subsequent divorce while still working together. Somehow we got through it and we remain close, but I have to say it was extremely difficult for both of us at various times.

You need to find a way to prevent relationship issues impacting on your business life. The key is to separate the two areas of your life. It isn't easy, especially if you also work together, so you need to work on it at a very conscious level.

I try to have a 'business head' and a 'home head'. When I step into my business I am the owner, the driver, the visionary, the person with whom the buck stops. At home I am a partner, a contributor, an equal and, most significantly, a human being, with all of the associated strengths and weaknesses. This separation of home and business roles has always worked well for me.

That said, I believe very strongly that you will never find balance in your life if you have unresolved problems in your relationship. Rather than rambling along, address the issues head-on and try to solve them. The longer they are left unchecked the more energy they will take from you (and your partner), and other areas of your life will lose their sparkle. Over time, it is easy to sink into a depressing and loveless relationship and life. Not a nice place to be.

What can I do today?

Are your relationship problems throwing your life out of balance? Ultimately, it will take much more energy to keep fighting than it will to address the issues, one way or another. Learning to separate your home life and your business life by changing your 'heads' can help but, more importantly, if you have a problem, find the courage to front it.

#34 If you lie down with dogs you get up with fleas

Throughout this book I have emphasised the importance of keeping negativity at bay as a mechanism for bringing balance back into your life. It is certainly one of the main themes, and for very good reason. Tip #18 introduced the idea of identifying those people who cause you problems and the importance of keeping them out of your life. This tip is an extension of this idea, focusing on identifying people that drain you of energy.

One of the surest ways to succeed in whatever it is you do is to surround yourself with positive, motivated and like-minded people. This doesn't happen by accident; it requires a very clear desire to achieve your goals, whatever they are, and the resolve to distance yourself from anyone who tries to steal your dreams.

I travel a lot and get to meet many people from all walks of life. Some are building massive empires, some are building small businesses from home. Yet the common topic of discussion is always the importance of having good people in your life to help you achieve your goals.

So what do I mean by good people? Put simply, it means those people who will support and encourage you to achieve your dreams no matter what. They will not try to talk you out of your dreams or let their own fears and insecurities come to the surface. Having people like this in your life is incredibly empowering and I believe they can help you to do anything you want.

When I wrote my first book, *101 Ways to Market Your Business*, and I was toying with the idea of trying to get it published, there were two kinds of people in my life. The first said, 'Go for it'—they believed in me and my passion. The second said, 'Don't waste your time—there are so many marketing books published already, you will never get yours published and it will only lead to disappointment'. For a while the dream-stealers had an influence on me, but luckily I didn't listen to them in the end.

Sadly, not everyone wants to see you achieve or grow. Even for those closest to you it can be a little scary. They may be afraid that they will lose you or that you will outgrow them. Others may feel resentful that you are achieving your goals when they are not.

From my experience, and from the amazing diversity of people that I am lucky enough to meet on a regular basis, I have come to believe in this above all else: surround yourself with powerful, dynamic and loving people who support you and your dreams, and your chances of achieving them will be increased dramatically. Otherwise, get yourself a good flea collar!

What can I do today?

Can you identify one person who really brings you down? Who always manages to find fault with everything in their life and yours, and every time you see them you dread the coming moanathon? Right here, right now, work out how you will get this person out of your life.

#35 Managing money issues

There are two kinds of businesses—those that have had money problems and those that will have money worries. It is a simple fact of doing business that sooner or later you will run into financial problems. A good friend of mine has been in business for over 30 years. About five years ago, at the age of 55, he almost went broke. I was amazed at how calmly he told me this story. Today he is the major shareholder and CEO of a company that turns over $300 million per annum. That is the fickle nature of business. I have had financial ups and downs over the years and I expect to have more. That said, I have learned a few things about dealing with money problems.

Here are a few of my tips for avoiding financial problems:

- Keep great records and enlist an excellent bookkeeper. Know exactly how much it costs to run your business each day, month and year. This gives you a target to aim for.
- Learn to manage your cash flow—it will break you if you don't manage it properly.
- Don't spend the money before it arrives. You haven't got it till it is in your account.
- Work out if you are making money on the products or services you are selling. You might think you are, but on closer inspection you may find that you are not.

If you do get into financial trouble, which means you are having difficulty paying your bills, these five tips will help you to get out of danger:

1. Be honest with yourself about the situation. Don't ignore it or believe that some magical event will happen to fix everything. The sooner you face it the better.
2. Get some advice. Professional advisors won't judge you, they are there to help. There are always options, even if it doesn't feel like it right now.

3. Talk to a friend or mentor in business—odds on they have been through the same thing and they may be able to give you some really practical and helpful information. Plus it helps to be able to talk about your problems.
4. Communicate to your creditors what the situation is and what you are doing about it.
5. Generally you will find that you have two very simple choices—reduce expenses or increase income. Ideally, do both. Having just two simple areas to focus on often makes managing the issues much easier.

And remember: worrying about money won't do much except give you an ulcer and turn your hair grey—it certainly won't make the money come in.

What can I do today?

If money isn't a problem, congratulations—but don't get too complacent. If you are seriously worried about money, follow my tips and do something about it. Believe me, you will feel much better knowing you are taking proactive steps to resolve the situation.

#36 Don't be afraid to sack some customers

One of the main reasons I chose to have my own business is so that I can decide who I do business with (and who I don't). Some people are just too much hard work as customers. Sometimes the old saying, 'the customer is always right', is really wrong.

Over the years that I have been consulting I have learned to be a good judge of character. When meeting potential clients for the first time I look at it as an interview—for them and for me. I listen to my gut instinct about the client. Are we on the same wavelength? Are they clear on what they want? Do I think we can work together? If I can't answer yes to these questions, then I prefer to be upfront and honest rather than try to make it work. So I suggest that they go elsewhere. It saves me a lot of time, energy and heartache in the long run.

Likewise there are times when a relationship with a client changes and no longer works. If they keep haggling over price, become unreasonably demanding or don't communicate effectively, it is time to move on. I have 'sacked' clients on a number of occasions. It was very satisfying and gave me a healthy sense of self-respect.

My marketing company used to have the advertising account for a large shopping centre. It was the account that everyone in town wanted. It was lots of work and carried enough prestige to make me feel good about it. But the client was extremely demanding, needing everything in very short and generally unrealistic time frames. They constantly bartered with us to get the work done cheaper and often they were very slow to pay.

So I did a review of the account and came up with some interesting realisations:

- We didn't actually make any profit out of the account.
- It stressed out everyone in the office.

- We couldn't take on more profitable work because all of our resources were tied up with this one account.
- We had no long-term security, as the client would not sign a contract.

Having done that review, I made the decision to resign the account. It was one of the smartest business moves I have ever made. I replaced this account with four new clients, generating four times the revenue for the same energy input. Don't get me wrong—to resign this account I was saying goodbye to over 70 per cent of the business's monthly income. But it was profitless volume, with little or no satisfaction, and ultimately I risked losing my best staff out of frustration with managing the account.

Some customers aren't worth having. If they cost you more in energy, time and satisfaction than they bring in, say goodbye, in the nicest possible way, of course.

What can I do today?

Do you have any customers that need to be sacked? Do a thorough review of those that are marginal and decide if it is costing too much for you to keep them. Give them a chance to change the situation, but don't be afraid to let them go.

#37 The torture of perfection

Being a perfectionist is hard work, and often those of us afflicted with this trait struggle when working with people who don't meet our expectations. I am certainly a perfectionist in many aspects of my work. I have tried to change but it just won't stick. However, it can be very draining (and unrealistic!) to try to make everything 100 per cent right all of the time.

Many small business owners are perfectionists. However, we must learn to compromise in some way, otherwise we'll drive ourselves—and those around us—insane.

As much as I struggle with the idea, sometimes near enough is good enough. It is simply too challenging to make every single aspect of a business perfect, especially when there are other people involved and their perception of what is acceptable is in all likelihood completely different from yours.

So how do we perfectionists overcome this issue? The following tips have worked for me:

- I always communicate very clearly what I expect in terms of the products and services that we deliver.
- I make a mental priority scale of what is really important and what is not, and I focus my perfectionist tendencies on the really important stuff.
- I have learned to accept that, while other people may do things differently, that doesn't mean they are wrong.
- I closely monitor customer feedback regarding quality control. This will tell me if things are slipping.
- Sometimes I just walk away—let the individuals do what they do and don't get involved.

It is great to be good at what you do. It is even better to be really committed to producing the very best quality products and services you can. But at some stage, you have to learn to let go and accept that perfection is nice, but excellence is OK.

What can I do today?

If you are a perfectionist this tip will have struck a chord with you. Try my tips and see if they work for you. The more you apply them the easier they will become and, most importantly, the more accepting you will become. Then you can use this excess energy to get a life!

#38 Do the work you love—give the rest to others

One of the most draining aspects of running a business can be doing the jobs you hate. We all have these dreaded tasks. Some may relate to the type of work you do, while others may be day-to-day tasks required to run the business.

I loathe bookwork, always have, always will. I have no desire to get all touchy feely with it and overcome my arch nemesis. Instead, I outsource it with very clear instructions on what I want and when I want it. I can't describe the relief I felt when I first outsourced my bookkeeping. Sure, there have been a few hiccups over the years, but far fewer than if I were doing it.

I believe that, as a business owner, you need to be able to do a bit of the picking and choosing in your life, even if the business is just you. Outsource what you don't like (and probably don't do very well anyway).

Often your role in the business changes as the business grows. You may have started out doing what you love, but now find yourself stuck in the office looking at spreadsheets instead of being on the floor and doing the work or dealing with the customers directly. You may need to rethink the way you run your business to get back to doing the things you really enjoy and are good at.

In order to get energised I need to work on challenging projects. For me, being pushed and challenged is really important for job satisfaction. Luckily I can pick and choose my projects, or sometimes they pick me.

I think more small business owners should give away the day-to-day tasks that drive them crazy, and instead spend their time making money and doing what they love. Now, how energising does that sound?

What can I do today?

Do you get to pick the good jobs? Do you try to do day-to-day tasks that drive you crazy? Today, decide what type of work you love and arrange it so that you do that. Then outsource or delegate any jobs that you are doing now that drive you crazy. You will benefit and so will your business.

#39 The more you give the more you get back

There is something really positive and energising about working with those less fortunate than ourselves or helping people in some way. I strongly recommend giving some of your valuable time to helping others. It serves a number of purposes, not the least of which is a reminder that your own life is not as bad as you sometimes may think it is.

Now I know that when you are struggling to find the time to spend with the family, or you are working 12 hours a day, the concept of spending time in a soup kitchen might seem a little crazy. But it is amazing therapy and you will be surprised how good it can make you feel.

Although this tip is about finding balance I would just like to add that I have met most of my largest clients while doing free work for various charity-based organisations. This is where you meet like-minded people. So while giving some of your time will definitely nurture your soul, you may even find that it gives the bank account a little nudge at the same time.

What can I do today?

Get involved in your community. Offer some time or resources within your business to help improve the quality of other people's lives. This will make you feel fantastic, make others respect you and your business, and will ultimately help to improve your business–life balance.

#40 Take off the medals—it shouldn't be that hard

There is a perception among business owners and even in the wider community that running a business is really hard —that you have to work long hours and, in all likelihood, make very little money. While I do agree with this at times, running a business shouldn't be like that, and it is up to us as business owners to change that perception, in both ourselves and others.

The notion that you deserve a medal for running your own business actively encourages this misery mentality. I see a lot of business owners complaining about the sacrifices they have made to have the business. Who cares? It was their choice in the first place. But get a group of business owners together and you've often got an instant moanathon, where all the woes of the small business world are aired, which helps to keep the notion in play.

It is good to be able to talk to other small business owners about the challenges we all face, but we need to balance this by also acknowledging the rewards we enjoy at the same time.

As small business owners we need to collectively change the way we think about what we do for a living. If we keep telling ourselves and others how tough it is, that's the way it will be. Every time you hear yourself starting the 'being a small business owner is really hard' speech, stop and change your mental wording. Feel free to discuss the challenges, but spend more time talking about the upside of being a business owner. It's interesting to see the impact that this has on other people: often they start to appreciate the positive aspects of their businesses much more.

So I am recruiting you to start challenging the perception that small business owners are a poor, tragic lot suffering great hardships, and concentrate on becoming the ideal of a powerful, in-control and successful small business owner.

What can I do today?

Write two lists. On one, note all the issues that you find challenging in your business, and on the other write down all of the rewards you enjoy. Next time you sense an opportunity to discuss how tough small business is, resist and talk about all of the positives. Over time it will become a habit that will make you feel better each time you hear the words leave your mouth.

Action page—What I need to do to regain balance in my life

----

6 | It's all about people and relationships

Relationships play a major role in adding to the day-to-day stress faced by most business owners. Spend a little time with any group of business owners and you will hear the same sorts of complaints about how hard it is to find good staff, how difficult customers are, that the family doesn't offer support and the suppliers continually fail to deliver on their promises.

In many cases relationships, or more specifically inability to manage relationships, can be the main cause of business stress. There are a host of courses to teach us how to balance our books but there aren't a lot of courses for business owners on how to build and keep good relationships.

This section looks at some of the most common relationship issues facing business owners and offers advice on how to overcome them. The messages can be applied to both professional and personal relationships.

#41   The power of expectations and how to manage them
#42   Do a relationship audit
#43   Understand that relationships have cycles and sometimes have to end
#44   The art of empathy
#45   Resolve issues quickly before they get out of hand
#46   Get out of your comfort zone—mix in new circles

#47 Building relationships takes time and energy
#48 Commit to becoming a communication guru
#49 Realise that other people may not share your enthusiasm towards your business
#50 Use counselling to resolve *any* relationship issue, not just issues between loved ones

#41 The power of expectations and how to manage them

When I was writing a book on customer service (*101 Ways to Really Satisfy Your Customers*), I spent a lot of time pondering the complex relationship between customers and businesses in an attempt to simplify the key aspects involved in this relationship. Building relationships with customers to ensure they keep coming back is the key to creating a successful business, and these are my three requirements for building exceptional relationships:

1. Know what your customer's expectations are.
2. Without failure, meet these expectations.
3. Where possible, exceed these expectations.

The surprising realisation for me is that virtually every relationship—not just that between business owner and customer—can be guided to success by following the same guidelines. The key step is the first requirement—knowing what their expectations are. If we don't know what people expect from us, how can we possibly give it to them? Generally we anticipate, guess and assume what others' expectations may be, but these are little more than stabs in the dark. Sometimes we might get it right, but more often we will get it wrong.

I have become a big believer in taking the time to properly clarify the expectations of anyone with whom I have a relationship. In most instances, this also gives me the opportunity to clarify my expectations (after all, these are relationships—it's a two-way street). A major cause of relationship breakdown is misunderstanding, usually resulting from a failure to clarify what the other person expects from the relationship or interaction.

For example, when I decide to run with a new supplier, I sit down with them, spell out what I expect from them in terms of quality control, adhering to time frames, response time to requests for quotes, and related issues. At the same time I clearly point out what we will do from our end in terms of payment terms, placing the order, reaching sales quotas, and so on. Then I reiterate in an email what we have agreed upon, so there is no room for misunderstanding. From here, all we have to do is meet each other's expectations and the relationship will be fine. Even if there is the odd hiccup, no harm will be done as long we both communicate openly and the incident is an exception rather than the norm.

What can I do today?

Do you define your expectations in relationships? Do you know what your expectations actually are? From today, take the time to clarify what you expect in relationships and what you will give in return. This deceptively simple tip can be applied to all relationships in your life.

#42 Do a relationship audit

Often we don't take the time to really think about our relationships with the people outside of our immediate family and close friends. By these I mean the relationships we have with staff, customers, suppliers, professional advisers, and so forth. Often we spend more time with these people than our families yet we don't really think the health of these relationships through.

A while back I made up a list of the key people in my professional and personal life. It was a long list, but I narrowed it down to the 20 most influential people. The list included family members, workmates, friends, suppliers, and so on. Next to each name I added three columns. In one column I wrote what I liked about the relationship, in the second column I noted problems in the relationship, and in the last column I described how I would like the relationship to change.

This exercise had a very significant impact on me and on these relationships. First, it made me take the time to stop and actually think about each of them. Second, it made me appreciate the aspects of the relationships that I liked. Importantly, it also let me put into words what I didn't like. And finally, it enabled me to clarify how I would like these relationships to evolve.

The end result has been more open and honest relationships with virtually everyone in my life. It is amazing how much stress can be removed from your life when you can fully express yourself. There are far fewer frustrations, confrontations and 'sticky moments'.

Often this simple act of analysis will solve many frustrations that you may be experiencing in a relationship. It works because your brain now has a way of understanding and translating the issues that have been causing you grief.

After some practice you may find that you can do a relationship audit in your head, without the need to write it down.

It is a quick and effective tool for clarifying why some relationships aren't working and what you need to do about it. Then you can start working towards making it happen.

What can I do today?

Make up a list of the most influential relationships in your life and do your own relationship audit on each of them. Once you have worked out exactly where these relationships are today, and where you would like them to be, you can start working towards making the necessary changes. If your list is too long, pick the top five to get started and work your way through the other names as your time and energy permit. Ideally, work towards being able to conduct a quick mental relationship audit.

#43 Understand that relationships have cycles and sometimes have to end

Most of us have experienced the warmth and passion of the early stages of a relationship, the trust and the security of a long-term relationship, and the sadness and sense of loss when a relationship ends. We know that personal relationships often follow these cycles.

Relationships have cycles because people change over time. The person you are today is most certainly different to the person you were ten years ago. As you change, sometimes you outgrow the people around you, to the point where you may find you have little in common with friends you may have had for years. Less effort is made to catch up and slowly the friendship fades away.

Just as our personal relationships go through these cycles, it's important to understand that the same principle applies to all of our relationships. While these changes don't necessarily mean that all relationships need to end, sadly some certainly do. The tricky part is knowing which ones need to end and which ones don't.

Personally, I don't like negative people and I do my utmost to keep them out of my life. When people enter a negative zone in their lives, I am understanding, but sometimes it reaches a point where I have to say enough is enough.

This may sound harsh, but we all need to be careful of getting caught up in negative, energy-sapping relationships. These people love having an ear to complain to. If you are surrounded by them, you will get dragged down. How can you have balance in your life if it is filled with negativity?

On a number of occasions I have 'sacked' clients (I talk about this in more detail in tip #36). The relationship was just too demanding, too one-sided and just plain hard. When this occurred I called the clients in, sat them down and explained that I didn't want to do their work anymore, for all of the above reasons. In each case I felt a great sense of self-respect and pride for having been strong enough to say that this relationship no longer serves me and that I don't want it or need it. Generally the client was shocked, but I am sure that most of them have heard it before, because they are difficult people in all that they do.

If you are struggling to find a sense of balance in your life, have a look at your relationships. Are some of the people closest to you obsessed with the misery of life, and always complaining? These could be customers, staff, suppliers, business partners or friends. Perhaps today is the day to sit down and say a few home truths about how you are feeling.

A word of warning: when these relationships end, they rarely end well. It won't be easy. You need to choose how you will finish a relationship that has reached its use-by date. You can let it die a slow, painful death or you can take control and nip it in the bud now. The point I want to make is that generally ending a negative relationship won't be easy.

What can I do today?

Look at the relationships in your life. Is there one particular relationship that is causing you a lot of grief and stress? Can this relationship be fixed? If not, how can you end it and get on with your life?

#44 The art of empathy

One of the best skills that I have learned that has not only helped me to build better relationships but also to reduce stress in my life is how to be more empathic. To me this means the ability to put myself in the shoes of the other person and look at the situation from their point of view.

It is an interesting exercise, and one that we all need to do a little more often, especially when we are feeling overwhelmed by events going on around us. When you make the conscious decision to think about a situation from the other person's perspective it takes you out of your own, stressed-out head and lets you see the situation in a way that may not have occurred to you before.

Being empathic generally makes us more compassionate, more understanding and more tolerant—not feelings we necessarily experience often in an increasingly chaotic world.

So, how do you become more empathic? Like most things in life worth learning, it takes some time and energy. If a difficult situation arises, instead of simply reacting with anger or frustration, stop and take a moment to start thinking empathically. Ask for time to think the matter over. Try to ignore your own feelings for a moment and look at the situation from the other person's perspective. How would you feel if you were in their shoes? Are their problems, complaints or actions reasonable? You might come full circle and end up back where you started, but at least you will have thought the situation through fully.

With empathy comes understanding, and I have learned this from some quite exceptional business people. It is the basic principle of great salesmanship; it is the force behind humanitarian movements the world over. Empathy is powerful stuff, but how does it help us to reduce stress and improve relationships? It shifts the centre of our universe (being us) to another point, and this gives us a very fresh view of the situation at hand.

Just as it is hard to feel pain when you laugh, it is hard to be stressed out and angry when you look at any situation with empathy. Try it—I guarantee that you will be surprised by how calming it is.

What can I do today?

Think about a relationship that is causing you a lot of stress at the moment. Now, you know how you feel about what is going on, but try to think about the problem from their point of view. How would you feel in the same situation? Are you being reasonable, or have you overreacted? Do you really understand the situation fully or do you need more information? By taking this empathic approach you will feel calmer, be more likely to resolve the situation and ideally be one step closer to finding some balance in your life.

#45 Resolve issues quickly before they get out of hand

At a difficult time in my marriage, my wife and I had fights that would last for days. Both of us would dish out the silent treatment, even long after we had forgotten the reason for the fight in the first place. Of course, I always thought I was right and Carolyne always thought she was right. Not a very good way to resolve an argument.

We sought the help of a psychiatrist to help us work through this issue. He walked us through the entire argument process and explained why neither of us was prepared to back down or surrender (it was a power struggle) even though the ongoing fights were making us both unhappy. Then he taught us a technique to stop conflict from escalating. It was surprisingly simple but the results were miraculous. I have since tried to use this approach in all areas of my life, not just at home.

The key is that one party needs to apologise first and fast— even if they do not believe they are the one in the 'wrong'. Now this can be tough to do, but believe me it gets easier the more often you do it. So each time Carolyne and I had an argument we took it in turns to be the first one to apologise. Importantly, we usually apologised within minutes of the argument starting. We could then actually talk about the issue in a calm and loving way, rather than letting the anger build and then blurting out hurtful things at each other.

The same principle applies to any kind of relationship, not just intimate relationships. If we let things stew and build, we tend to explode rather than explain. It is much better to raise an issue early, as soon as it appears. Try not to assign blame— put the issue out there first and then work together for ways to resolve it. It really does work.

A lot of stress and angst results from a sense of not being able to express how you are feeling because you are afraid of having an argument that could get out of control. Open and honest dialogue is essential, and this can only happen when you act quickly and unemotionally. A much better option than going on a tirade after a few drinks at the Christmas party because you have reached boiling point.

While my marriage didn't last, Carolyne and I are very close friends to this day and talk often about this defusing process and the way it continues to make our lives and our relationships better.

What can I do today?

Are issues building between you and someone close to you? Does this stress you out and add to an overall sense of dissatisfaction with life? Defuse the situation today before it gets any worse. Sit down with the person and talk about the issues as you see them, and try to work through a way to resolve them and move on with your life.

#46 Get out of your comfort zone — mix in new circles

If you want to make small changes in your life, a few adjustments here and there should do it. But if you feel that your life is so out of balance and out of control that you could just scream, little nudges just won't do. If you want to make big changes in your life, you will need to start doing things very differently.

Remember that you don't just get out of bed one day to find that your life is so out of balance that it feels like your world is collapsing. These problems will have built up over time. Many factors in your life will have played a part. In particular, the people around you have a huge impact on your state of mind and emotional wellbeing.

How do you know if you have the wrong kind of people in your life? If they have been around for years they will feel really comfortable, like a well worn pair of jeans, even if deep down you know that you don't look as good in them as you did ten years ago.

The best way to find out if you have the right people in your life is to meet others and do a comparison. Break out of the old, safe routines and patterns that have got you to this difficult point and start to expand your horizons. You have to get out of your comfort zone and meet new people.

Of course, when you feel like your life is out of control the last thing you will want to do is spend time expanding your circle of friends, associates and business contacts. You will find a million reasons not to break out of your comfort zone, but now is the time to make the effort to change things in your life.

When my business was at its most out of control I joined a gym—and went three times a week. It was great to be surrounded by motivated, energetic people all trying to improve themselves and get more out of life. This started to rub off on me. Soon I was much more energised and positive in every interaction I had with people. I had more enthusiasm for what I was doing and I most certainly managed to think a heck of a lot clearer. There are only upsides—financially, and in your health and happiness—to mixing with a new circle of people.

So, depending on what aspect of your life you need to get back under control, get out, meet new people and you will be astonished by the effect a fresh perspective will have on your life.

What can I do today?

Identify one way to meet new people, whether it be for your business or social life, and commit to it. It may feel a little awkward and uncomfortable at first, but work through that and see what comes out at the other end.

#47 Building relationships takes time and energy

Most people know that building better relationships requires a commitment of time and energy. But when you are stressed out, working really long hours, under financial pressure and struggling to stay on top of things, the idea of taking time out to build relationships just keeps slipping down your list of priorities.

One example of this is delegation. Clearly, if you can delegate some of your responsibilities life will become a little easier, but it takes time to delegate and to teach other people the skills or the systems required to take on particular tasks. In the midst of a typically crazy day you probably think, 'It will be easier to do it myself'. So that is what you do, taking on more and more responsibility every day until you reach breaking point.

I know first hand how easy it is to prioritise tasks over people. I tend to start work earlier than everyone else in my business. It gives me a little quiet time before the phone starts to ring and the demands of the day kick in. From about 8 a.m. my team starts to arrive. They like to drop into my office to say hello and have a chat about the day ahead. This used to drive me crazy—I had already been working for at least an hour and was trying to beat the clock to get things done. I came to dread the sound of the front door of the office opening because I knew that it meant I would spend the next hour being distracted.

I looked at this hour as a waste of my time, but I also knew that the people I worked with needed the interaction, some social chitchat and a chance to ask questions and plan for the day ahead. In spite of this, I was getting more and more frustrated until one day my frustration reached overload. At this point I knew that I had to change my attitude and decided to look at this one hour as an opportunity, not an irritation. I decided that every day from 8 a.m. till 9 a.m. I wouldn't plan anything other than meeting and greeting my team, planning the projects for the day ahead and generally getting to know everyone a little better. I decided to enjoy this time instead of resenting it. And what a change this has made. Now I look forward to everyone arriving, communication works at a much higher level, projects run more smoothly, issues are sorted out faster, and we all feel much closer.

Again, the shift required is a mental one. Look at the time spent building relationships as an investment, not a chore. The stronger your relationship with your customers the more loyal they will be. The stronger your relationship with your staff the more likely they will do the extra things that will make your life easier.

Regardless of the desired outcome, a relationship of any sort is like a flower: it takes time and the right environment to grow. Look at the time and energy spent building relationships as an investment in you.

What can I do today?

Do you have any situations in your life that you could turn from a perceived waste of time to an opportunity to build stronger relationships? This could relate to your staff, your suppliers, your customers or your family. The change required is internal. It will take some adjustments and you may slip up from time to time. Remind yourself why you are making the time to build these relationships and understand that it is part of bringing your business and your life back into balance.

#48 Commit to becoming a communication guru

I love communication—written, visual, oral, the lot. I have always been extremely passionate about understanding the role of communication in both my professional and personal life.

Communication is the key to many of the tips in this book, and I have observed time and time again that successful business owners are good communicators. They may be good talkers, good writers, good listeners or all three, but the end result is that people enjoy their company and they tend to attract good people into their lives.

So what has this got to do with balancing your business and your life? Put simply, the more effectively you can communicate the more manageable your relationships will become. If you can build effective relationships with customers, staff and everyone you deal with on a daily basis, ultimately every aspect of your life will become less stressful.

So, the challenge is to become a better communicator. How do you go about this? There are a number of ways. First, there are many excellent books on the topic. As mentioned elsewhere in this book, the one I love the most is Dale Carnegie's *How to Win Friends and Influence People*—a classic book with a not-so-classic title. If you only read one book, let it be this one (I read it every year at Christmas). It will teach you more about communication than any other book on the market. There are many other excellent books on body language, presenting, writing and everything in between. Refer to the recommended reading section at the back of this book for some suggestions. There are also websites available that specialise in improving communication at every level.

In addition, there are courses available on communication, both privately and in government-run organisations. These tend to address specific areas, but any way of improving your communication skills can only have positive benefits.

Becoming a better communicator will affect your business on many levels and have a flow-on effect. Working on communication will help to bring your life and your business back into equilibrium.

What can I do today?

Commit to improving your communication skills. Start by buying Dale Carnegie's famous book or enrolling in a public speaking course. There are lots of options to choose from, but the most important part is making the commitment today.

#49 Realise that other people may not share your enthusiasm towards your business

Obsessiveness about what we do is often disguised as passion, a characteristic that we admire in people. Business owners tend to become a little obsessed with their businesses, and as a result their lives—and their conversation—start to revolve around the business. Unfortunately, their family and friends may not share the desire to talk incessantly about the business. For some business owners this can at first be a little hurtful—why can't they share our enthusiasm?

As a serial entrepreneur who simply can't help himself, I have learned to recognise the telltale sign when people's eyes start to glaze over as I wax lyrical about a project that I am working on (the sound of snoring is also a dead giveaway). I use this as a reminder that not everyone shares the same degree of passion about developing a marketing plan for a law firm as I do, and that maybe it is time to get out of my business a little and back into the real world.

It is important to have some positive outlets for the stress of running a business. Holding on to stress is one reason that we get out of balance in the first place. But you need to pick the place, the time and the people. Make sure there are people in your life who you *can* talk to about your business and that there are other people who are just friends, who love you for who you are, not what you do.

I try to go camping at least once a year with a few friends, each of whom owns their own business. One is a security guard, one is a plumber and one is a handyman. Surprisingly, when we go camping we talk about fishing, the weather, sport, politics, girls and just about any other topic apart from our businesses. This is very therapeutic for each of us. If I have business issues that I need to talk about, I have other friends I can talk to.

Don't get upset when other people don't share your enthusiasm; instead, use it as a reminder to have a life outside of your business. Be aware of what is going on in the world and in other people's lives. It will be better for you and your business in the long run.

What can I do today?

Since becoming a business owner, have you lost a number of friends because you are too busy to make time to socialise? Pick up the phone, reconnect and remember that there is a lot more to life other than your business. Taking your mind off your business for a while is a very positive thing to do, and you will be able to return to your responsibilities recharged.

#50 Use counselling to resolve *any* relationship issue, not just issues between loved ones

People often think of relationship counselling as only applicable to couples with marital issues, but counselling can be helpful for any relationship. One of the greatest frustrations in dealing with a troubled relationship is not knowing how to fix it. We assign blame (it can't be my fault!), we get defensive, hurt and angry. It's very difficult to resolve a situation from this position.

A neutral third party offering simple, practical advice can really work wonders. They can take the emotion out of the situation and make it more analytical. I know that I don't have the skills to understand or resolve every relationship issue so, just as I would see a lawyer with a legal issue, I see a psychologist or counsellor for a people issue.

Several years ago I sold part of my company to a long-time friend (who used to be my boss), Neil Swann. We were both a little concerned about working together, worried that it might damage a very strong friendship. We also knew that we needed a strategy to help us resolve the issues that can arise in any business. So, we enlisted the help of a mutual (but independent) friend, Phil Colbert.

Phil was given the role of mediator, confidant and advisor and, most importantly, the deciding vote on issues that Neil and I could not agree upon. We had a contract drawn up accordingly. Now we have a mechanism for resolving issues if they arise. We haven't yet needed to call on Phil, but simply having a plan in place to deal with any problem that might arise is very reassuring.

There are people who can help you to work through relationship problems, whether in your professional or personal life. This will remove a lot of stress and angst from your day-to-day life, which will in turn let you get on with running your business and achieving your dreams and aspirations.

What can I do today?

Are there any relationships in your life that need work? Where could you get professional advice? As a starting point, look in the Yellow Pages under 'Relationship counselling'. A counsellor will be just as happy to talk to you about a professional relationship as a personal relationship. Make that appointment today.

Action page—What I need to do to regain balance in my life

----

7 | Nurture the mind, the body and the soul

At conferences and seminars people often ask me what is the best thing they can do to build their business and to make it more successful. My advice is very simple—have a holiday. In fact I give this advice so often I am thinking about opening up a travel agency! From my experience and observation, to have a truly successful business you need to work less on the business and more on yourself.

If you are stressed out, exhausted, unwell, worried and totally out of control, how can you possibly build a successful and dynamic business? And what price will you have paid in the attempt?

In Section 2 we discussed the retraining process, and how to start working towards achieving balance by undoing bad habits in all aspects of your life. In this section we look in more detail at what you can do to nurture your mind, body and soul.

#51   Do you take your body for granted?
#52   Baby steps to get started
#53   Enlist outside help—why not use a personal trainer?
#54   Make movement a part of your life
#55   Increase airflow—in your body, in your workplace and in your life
#56   Guilt-free pampering

#57   Respect yourself enough to take the time to look your best
#58   Yoga—feeling like a pretzel is not as bad as it sounds
#59   Invest in good slumber
#60   Develop your own style of meditation

#51 Do you take your body for granted?

For many years I would have answered this question with a resounding yes. I didn't think about my body or my health terribly much, and it showed. My main focus was always on my business—how to work more, achieve more, get more done and earn more money to make ends meet. All of my energy and attention were given to my business, and very little was spared for my own health and wellbeing.

While today younger entrepreneurs are generally more aware and in tune with health issues, I still believe that a large proportion of the small business community really don't look after themselves very well. We need our bodies to be strong and fit to help us achieve our goals. So why do so many of us treat our bodies so badly?

When you are in survival mode, you block out most things except the need to make ends meet and get as much work done as you can. This can often go on for many years. It becomes habit-forming, and these habits are hard to break. Life becomes so full and busy, with so many demands from so many areas, that finding time for yourself is impossible, or so you think.

But you can only take your body for granted for so long. Abuse it and you will ultimately pay the price. The healthier you are mentally, physically and spiritually the better every aspect of your life will become.

From my own experience it is simply a matter of adjusting your priorities. Is your health and wellbeing a priority or not? I have a list of the five most important things in my life. I keep this at the front of my diary and in my wallet (for those times I forget or lose focus). Treating my body with respect is at the top of the list.

What can I do today?

Stop and take a moment to appreciate just how amazing your body is. Appreciate it for what it does every single day despite the enormous pressure you put on it. Most importantly, commit to looking after it and treating it with respect. Is being healthy at the top of your priority list or at the bottom? Decide today whether your priorities need to change.

#52 Baby steps to get started

I know that at times it can be irritating to be told all the ways you need to change. Sometimes we take it personally; sometimes we point the finger and say, 'Well, you're not perfect, why should I listen to you?' Change is a traumatic process for many people, and this book is designed to give you some simple tips to make the process a little easier.

You can't change habits of a lifetime in a few days. I put on a lot of weight over ten years and it has taken me four years to lose most of it. One of the best lessons that I have learned to help with the process is the importance of baby steps. If you try to change everything today you will fail.

To address issues relating to business–life balance—from losing weight, eating healthier and getting fitter to working fewer hours, removing stress and building better relationships—I ask myself six questions:

1. Where am I today?
2. Where do I want to be?
3. What do I need to do to get there (big picture)?
4. What can I do to get there in baby steps?
5. Who do I need to help me?
6. How will I know when I have made it?

While each part of the process is important, I have found that baby steps are a subtle but crucial component. Ask anyone who hasn't exercised for a while to run ten kilometres and they will either refuse to do it or attempt it and die in the process. But ask them to go for a 30-minute walk and they are more likely to do it. It isn't a big jump from there to a one-hour walk, then to a ten-minute run, then a 30-minute run and ultimately an hour run—maybe they will run ten kilometres in that hour. The key is breaking the goal into smaller chunks that are achievable.

There is a great saying that I heard recently: 'How do you eat an elephant? One mouthful at a time.' While on this theme, imagine weighing 200 kilograms and having a doctor tell you that you have to lose 120 kilograms. How daunting is that? Especially when after one week you have lost only two kilograms. Yet if you break down your goal into baby steps—aiming to lose weight in, say, six stages of 20 kilograms each—you will find it much easier to achieve your goal.

For many people, getting larger projects started is much easier if you can break them into small manageable pieces, but there are other benefits, including the sense of satisfaction from reaching milestones more often. In fact this is often enough to keep people motivated to battle on.

This is really just basic project management: break any large and ambitious project into small, more manageable components, which aren't as daunting to start. When they built the Great Wall of China it is unlikely that a million semi-trailers pulled up with bricks and an army of bricklayers just started putting it together. More likely it was approached one section at a time and, block by block, one of the most amazing structures in the world was built.

Apply this rule to any big change you need to make to your life. Start by thinking big and then break your goal down into baby steps to make it manageable.

What can I do today?

If you are feeling daunted by making changes in your life simply due to the sheer size of the changes required, try the process described above. For each goal, break the change into baby steps that you feel comfortable with and that you are confident you can achieve. Your chances of success may be greatly increased.

#53 Enlist outside help—why not use a personal trainer?

So you've adjusted your priorities and decided to take baby steps towards a healthier, more energetic you. I did this, but I needed one more weapon to ensure that I really got moving—a personal trainer. In this age of outsourcing, why not enlist the sheer energy, enthusiasm and motivation a good personal trainer can offer to assist you in your own balance battle.

I am a firm believer in personal trainers, having experienced exceptional results first hand. But not all personal trainers are the same and finding the right one for you might take a few attempts. A few years back I did one session with a male personal trainer who spent 40 minutes telling me how fat and unfit I was, all the while trying to chat up the girl on the machine next to us. I was humiliated and really angry.

I am surprised that I ever went near a gym or a personal trainer again. But luckily I did and, as mentioned earlier in the book, I now have two personal trainers (one just wasn't enough), and we have been working together for almost four years. The experience of working with my trainers, Sam and Kelly, was completely different to my earlier experience with the jerk.

First they sat me down and gave me a complete and thorough evaluation. They really got to know me and what I wanted to achieve. They asked about my lifestyle, my business and the demands on my time, what type of exercise I liked and what I didn't like, how I ate, when I ate, my emotional state, my motivational buttons, and so on. Then we set about working together on fixing what they considered were my main issues. The first issue was *when* I was eating (see tip #65, Get your day off to a healthy start)—no more mornings fuelled only by coffee! They insisted I must eat a healthy breakfast every day. I started doing gentle yoga and light gym work with weights, working up to more active cardiovascular work.

I couldn't imagine life without them. Forget any stereo-typical images you may have of a drill sergeant yelling and screaming at some poor sod (in this instance you) to do another 30 push-ups. A good personal trainer will motivate you, encourage you, challenge you, make allowances for when you feel down, and share your passion to reach your goals.

Every few months I sit down with my trainers and we review where we are at and how I am feeling. It really is all about me. There are times when I am on the road for weeks at a time and they ring to check that I am OK and that I am getting in some exercise. They have taught me to only ever stay in hotels that have well-equipped gyms, how to do yoga in confined spaces such as hotel rooms or on a plane, how to eat out and not blow the diet, and so much more.

While I train we laugh, we joke, we share good times and sad times. Along the way we have become very close friends. They have seen me at my lowest point physically, and they have been there for some of my greatest tribulations. They have also shared in my sense of accomplishment at each milestone, and I acknowledge that without them I wouldn't have achieved what I have.

If you need a little help to get your mind, body and soul on track, a personal trainer who is a real professional, to whom you can relate and who communicates well with you is an amazing asset. Take the time to find the right one (or two) for you.

What can I do today?

If you are really serious about getting your body healthier, and part of that process involves getting physically fit, get a personal trainer to help you. Shop around, find one who you like and who you think can motivate you in the right way, and commit to doing a set number of sessions. Use them for advice on healthy eating, and stress relief and management, as well as to guide you on the road to getting fit.

#54 Make movement a part of your life

In an age when so much effort goes into making us do less physically, no wonder we find it hard to get moving. We spend hours sitting in front of large television screens and home theatres, surfing the net and playing electronic games, as well as long hours at work, often with little or no physical movement involved. Yet our bodies are made for movement, not to sit still. Back when humans lived in caves, the only time they weren't moving was when they were asleep. The rest of the time there would be this little thing called the battle for survival to keep them on their toes.

I have spoken about change, about treating your body with respect and the benefits of a healthier lifestyle. Making movement—even the smallest and simplest of movements—a part of your life will really help.

Every day, think about what you are doing to see if there is a way that you could increase your level of activity. For most of us the most obvious place to start is with our cars. Perhaps you tend to get a little lazy and drive to the shop, even though it's only a ten-minute walk away. Maybe you tell yourself that you don't have the time to walk. Why not? Let's make more time and slow things down a little, just to get you moving again.

Using the stairs instead of a lift or escalator is another really easy way to move and it only takes a bit of extra effort for a short amount of time. Arrange to meet a friend to go for a walk instead of a meal. It is surprising how many people are more than happy to do this.

There are many ways to get more active. A little effort here and a little there will make a bigger difference than you realise. Most of the difference occurs in your head when you change the habit of thoughtlessly reaching for the car keys. Once you start to get more movement in your life your body will start to respond and like it a lot. From there the level of movement can be increased. The more you move, the more relaxed you will feel and the closer you will be to finding balance in your life.

What can I do today?

When you grab your car keys, stop and think for a second—can you do this trip on foot (or by bike, rollerblades, swimming or hopping)? If you can, why don't you? Ask yourself this question every time you pick up your car keys from now on.

#55 Increase airflow—in your body, in your workplace and in your life

A side effect of sitting at desks all day and being less active is that we have forgotten how to breathe properly—that is to say, taking big deep breaths in and out. The same applies to many jobs, not just desk jobs. Doing yoga, exercising and laughing, among other things, will all help to get that air flowing in and out a little better. I think of my breathing similarly to the way I think of the food and drink that I put in my body. The better the quality, the more beneficial it will be to me. While we can only make limited changes to the quality of the air around us, we can make dramatic changes to how we breathe.

We give very little thought to our breathing; slumped over a desk or in front of the TV you might be surprised to realise that you are taking only shallow breaths. Every once in a while your body cries out for more oxygen and you take a really deep breath—have you ever noticed how good that feels? You get rid of the old stale air, your posture improves and you feel energised. As a bonus, you feel more relaxed and calm. How nice it would be to feel like this all the time!

So, if we breathe deeper we feel energised, calm and relaxed, we sit up straight and we get a nice warm feeling in our body. All of this and it's free. Sounds to me like something we all need to do a lot more often.

But ideally you want to breathe the best air possible. Recycled air-conditioned air probably doesn't fall into that category. I suggest doing as much as you can to get fresh air circulating in your workplace and in your home. That isn't easy in some buildings, but do what you can.

Flowers have a wonderful way of making air feel good—I can't really explain what I mean and I don't have any scientific proof for this, but I sense that a room with flowers in it just smells and tastes better. Unconsciously this makes you breathe more deeply. At the opposite end of the scale it is harder and less pleasant to breathe deeply in a dusty, stale or bad-smelling room. Do what you can to create a positive airflow and your breathing will improve dramatically.

If you can't get the air into you, the next best thing is getting yourself out into the air, so go outside and take those deep breaths on a regular basis throughout the day.

What can I do today?

Become more conscious of airflow—directly, through your own breathing, and in the environment around you. Sit up straight, take ten deep, slow breaths in and out. Do this as often as you can throughout the day. Also look at ways of improving the air in your workplace and at home. Open windows, turn on fans, freshen rooms and get rid of dust. Air is more important than food and water.

#56 Guilt-free pampering

Pampering means different things to everyone, but at its simplest it's something that makes us feel good. That alone is good reason to be pampered every once in a while.

First of all, figure out how you like to be pampered. For example, is a day in a health spa your ideal pampering experience? Being worked on from head to toe, rubbed, scrubbed and oiled up, every muscle massaged and washed off? If it is, why not do it regularly?

You'll probably come up with excuses straightaway as to why you shouldn't. Your first thought is probably that you can't afford to do it all the time. Fair enough, it is not a cheap exercise, but is it really that expensive? How much are your own wellbeing, sense of calm and overall sanity worth? We need to see pampering ourselves as a form of investment and, in my opinion, one that has exceptional returns.

Your second argument is probably that you don't have the time—don't you think that's all the more reason to make time? Generally there is never enough time, or a good time to do the things we need to help us to feel more peaceful and calm. Our own needs end up on the bottom of the very long 'to do' list, and this needs to change.

Finally, you will say that you feel guilty spending a day away from the business getting pampered. Now that last one is a shocking excuse. If your business can't survive for a day without you being there, then you haven't got a business—you've got a jail sentence.

If taking a whole day off is too much to contemplate, try breaking it into baby steps and organise to come in late one morning. Spend that time before work doing something that really nurtures you and makes you feel wonderful. For example, I often get up early and go for a drive to a beautiful creek about 40 minutes from my place. I go for a swim, sit and watch the birds and the rainforest wake up, then head home for a shower and to get ready for work. On days when I do this I generally get to work about 10 a.m., but I feel incredible.

Overcome the guilt of pampering yourself by breaking it into stages that you are comfortable with. Then figure out how you really like to be pampered. Be selfish, be honest, be decadent—it doesn't matter. It is all about you. Take a few hours off in the middle of the day to see a movie, have a golf day once every few weeks, do a course in something not related to your work, donate some time at the local animal shelter, go to the gym—whatever does it for you.

Be prepared to pamper yourself often. You deserve it.

What can I do today?

Do you know how you like to be pampered? Make up a list of the top five things you love to do that could be considered pampering. Then make a date for each of them. No ifs and no buts. Just do it.

#57 Respect yourself enough to take the time to look your best

I am a big believer in the importance of personal grooming and appearance. Investing time, money and energy in how you look shows a sense of self-respect.

Often, as people get really overworked, exhausted and run-down, personal grooming and appearances start to slide. Men stop shaving as often, they wear creased shirts and scuffed, dirty shoes. The same lowering of standards applies to women, but I am not a brave enough man to go into specifics! We all simply run out of energy and something has to give.

Many years ago I did a series of courses to become a SCUBA diving instructor. I was fortunate enough to have a great mentor at the time, a huge man by the name of Bob Baldwin. I remember him looking me in the eye and saying, 'If you want people to respect you, dress like you respect yourself.' I have found this to be very true. If you take the time to dress well and groom yourself, people are more likely to extend you courtesy and respect. They also listen to what you have to say—which is why police and military personnel have to comply with such exacting standards in terms of uniform and personal grooming.

As part of your battle to regain control of your life, can you spare some time to ensure you look the part? Is your suit really old, out of date and moth-eaten? Is it time to let the combover go and be proudly bald? If you aren't sure, find some friends who you can trust to be really, really honest and ask for their opinion. We all need a bit of a makeover from time to time. This rule can be extended to other parts of your life and business as well. Is your car dusty all the time? Is your office in need of a good spring clean?

This tip is simple—give yourself enough time to spend on grooming and appearance. The better you look, the better you will feel, and the more in control and confident you will be. If it means new clothes, so be it. If it means a new hairdo, go for it. Invest in yourself; there's never a good time or enough money, so today is as good a day as any.

What can I do today?

Make the commitment to review your overall appearance. Does it need work? Do you need help? Make a list of the things you need to do to improve the way you look (and feel), and go for it. Give yourself enough time each day to get ready properly. It will make a big difference to how the rest of your day pans out.

#58 Yoga—feeling like a pretzel is not as bad as it sounds

I don't want to be melodramatic, but yoga really did change my life. It is an amazingly therapeutic activity that can be done by people from eight to 80 (and beyond). From the really unfit to top athletes, yoga can be equally challenging to both.

Yoga has Hindu roots, dating back many thousands of years. It is a series of postures and breathing exercises practised to gain control of the body and the mind in order to achieve tranquillity. It stretches muscles, aligns the spine, massages the internal organs and clears the brain. It truly is a magical cure-all, and I have never felt as good in my life as when I do yoga on a regular basis.

You don't need any special equipment, as generally all aids are supplied in class. Wear a t-shirt and shorts or other comfortable clothing. Classes vary dramatically in exertion level—from restorative and very gentle to hard-core Ashtanga yoga, which will have you sweating profusely in minutes. I strongly recommend that anyone doing yoga for the first time go to a beginners' class. Forget ego; yoga is not about that. Just start at the easiest level and work your way up.

It is surprising how many people go to yoga for stress relief. I see a lot of familiar faces each week, and many of them own their own small businesses. Many business owners I know sneak off during the day to go to a yoga class—an excellent investment in health and wellbeing and in their business.

I love going to a class and looking around the room: there are young people, old people, really fit people, terribly unfit people, skinny people, fat people, men, women, boys and girls. It is truly a melting pot for people from all walks of life. After a yoga class I always sleep really well, my mind is clear of all chatter and my body feels great. I wake up the following morning feeling like a new man.

OK, OK. You get the point. Yoga is amazing. If the only thing you got out of this book was a desire to go and do one yoga class, then I would be very, very happy. Talk to people who do yoga, sit in on a couple of easy classes, have an open mind and see if yoga works for you.

What can I do today?

Sign up for a series of introductory yoga classes (check your local newspaper, telephone directory or gym). It will change your life.

#59 Invest in good slumber

The best investment I have made in many years (apart from a sojourn in India) is buying a magnificent bed. Taking a very close friend of mine who happens to be a chiropractor bed shopping was a costly exercise, but it has certainly been worth it.

I'd had the same bed for as long as I could remember. I often used to laugh when I saw the indentation that my less-than-slender body had left in the mattress after years of prolonged use, but I never really understood how badly it was affecting me.

So Dr Debra Lawson took me to the bed shop, muttering under her breath about the state of my bed and throwing in words like 'hunchback' and 'crippled' throughout the process. We stopped beside the second most expensive bed in the store and she simply told me I had to buy this one. It's made of state-of-the-art latex, weighs the same as a jumbo jet and is very, very comfortable.

After the first few nights in my new bed I woke up with really bad backaches. Dr Deb explained that this was due in no small part to my spine and associated muscles going back to their rightful places and realigning. But after that first week I began to have the most deep, restful and rejuvenating sleeps I have ever had in my life. I have to say, I love my bed. If my apartment was on fire the mattress would go out the window first and then whoever else happened to be there with me.

Like so many other aspects of a busy person's life, sleep becomes simply one item on the list of things to do. The problem is that if you don't sleep well you don't really get the chance to recharge your body. The more stressed out and demanding your life is, the more important the role of sleep. Do everything in your power to make sure you get enough. So, apart from having the world's greatest bed, here are some of my tips for a great night's sleep:

- Make your bedroom really comfortable, peaceful and soothing.
- Don't eat heavy meals late at night (you never sleep as well on a full stomach and often have very broken sleep).
- Install good quality, heavy curtains or blinds so your bedroom is dark.
- Buy good quality bed linen. The nicer your bed feels the better you will sleep.
- Don't drink too much (certainly no tea or coffee) late at night.
- Don't force yourself to stay awake. When the waves of sleep start, go to bed.
- Don't watch television or work on your laptop in bed.
- Before you go to sleep, spend a few minutes taking big, deep and slow breaths. You will feel refreshed for a few minutes, then go off to a deep slumber.
- Long before you go near your bed, work out what you are doing the next day and start mentally shutting down for the night.
- Have a good hot shower before getting into bed. For some reason sleeping is easier when you are clean, and a hot shower is really relaxing. Your body temperature will start to drop after a hot shower, helping you to drift off.

Having a really good sleep every night of the week is a great personal investment. Spend the money, make sure the environment is right and enjoy the benefits.

What can I do today?

How is your bed? Is it long overdue for an upgrade? Is today the day where you go and buy that new, state-of-the-art bed that will have a dramatic effect on how you sleep and how you feel? Enjoy the buying process and look at it as an excellent investment in the new calm, in-control and balanced you.

#60 Develop your own style of meditation

Meditation is one of those things that some people think is really 'out there'; others have tried it and haven't really been able to do it properly; some think it is a bunch of baloney; and others swear by it as an amazingly recuperative practice. I have held each of those views at different stages in my life.

Today I think meditation is an exceptional tool for helping to calm a full, or in many cases overfull, brain. It is a way of slowing down, gaining focus, putting issues into perspective and restoring and revitalising.

So what is meditation? The dictionary defines it as 'quiet contemplation', and that is really what it is all about. It is a process of slowing down the mind, getting all of the distractions and racing thoughts out, and simply focusing on one main thought, idea or problem.

We very rarely get to contemplate one thing at a time in today's frantic world. As discussed throughout this book, stress is the result of huge demands on individuals, the never-ending push and pull of daily life. Meditation is a mini vacation away from this.

So how do you meditate? A good question and a tough one to answer. Like virtually every activity related to wellbeing, there are vastly different definitions and descriptions. For me, meditation involves simply finding a quiet place, making yourself comfortable, then taking deep breaths in and out, thinking about one thing and one thing only. It is hard to do and the mind wants to race all over the place like crazy. The battle is to keep it focused; it will take time to learn and develop this skill. You might do it for just five minutes to get started. You might fall asleep. I call this a 'mini meditation'.

I am sure there are die-hard meditation Nazis who would be aghast at this description, but really, even the simplest of meditations has to be better than nothing. There are many places where you can go and learn to meditate with a group.

I have tried a number—some good, some not. What beginners need are lessons; someone talking you through the process really does help. To sit in a group, chanting and 'ohmming' for an hour while sitting with your legs crossed is very hard for a beginner.

Meditate to suit you. If you like it and you want to learn more, you will certainly find places and organisations to help you. If you are content to do your own 'mini meditations' they will certainly help you, and you will grow to really enjoy these times of quiet contemplation and reflection.

What can I do today?

Do your first 'mini meditation' today. If you like it, try to do it once a day, either first thing in the morning or when you get home from your business. You will grow to love it.

Action page — What I need to do to regain balance in my life

----

8 | Use the right fuel to create calm

This section is very relevant to me as, up until a few years ago, my weight and overall wellbeing had always been connected to my level of stress. When I was stressed out my weight went up; when I was relaxed my weight went down. In recent years I have lost around 40 kilograms. This took a lot of effort; for a start, I had to reprogram my eating habits considerably. Now, for the first time in my life, my weight and stress levels are not related. This is a constant challenge and one that I have accepted I will have to work on for the rest of my life.

Travelling around the country and speaking at conferences, I meet a lot of very stressed out and unhealthy business owners. They work really long hours, they are under huge pressure, they don't exercise, they eat poorly and generally have a very bad lifestyle, mainly because of their dedication to their business. This is all the more ironic since most of them had assumed that running their own business would give them the time and money to live a more enjoyable, relaxed life, which it can do but often doesn't.

One thing I do know for certain is that if I eat well and treat my body with respect and gratitude it will help me to achieve everything I want to in my life—and that is a long list. Being aware and conscious of what I eat and drink is an essential part of regaining a healthy body and a balanced life; for me, as for many people, it is a work in progress.

This section will help those readers who want to feel healthier. It is based on my own experiences and challenges in this area of my life.

#61   Keep a diary of what you eat and when
#62   Alcohol, coffee, nicotine, sugar ... what's your drug of choice?
#63   What exactly does eating well mean?
#64   Learn to enjoy food again
#65   Get your day off to a healthy start
#66   Water water everywhere
#67   Eating out doesn't need to be unhealthy
#68   Encourage healthy eating in your workplace
#69   When it comes to food, always be prepared
#70   The 80 per cent rule—let your hair down from time to time

#61 Keep a diary of what you eat and when

We are often unconscious of the relationship between stress and food. Some people stop eating when they are stressed; others eat more when they are under the hammer. As a general rule, and from my own experience, when people's lives get out of balance, so do their eating habits. They start to eat poorly, favouring junk food and quick energy fixes or 'pick me ups' instead of more wholesome and nutritious fare.

I know this as I lived like this for many years. It is a vicious cycle because the worse you eat, the worse you tend to feel and the more you crave the foods that are not good for you. The human brain does a great job of softening this blow for us by justifying what we eat, and we simply go into the world of denial.

A few years back I was wondering why I couldn't lose weight. On the suggestion of a good friend I started a food diary to see exactly what I was eating and drinking every day. I soon noticed that I was drinking quite a lot of tea and coffee, about ten cups a day. Now, in each cup I would have two teaspoons of sugar. That adds up to one hundred and forty teaspoons of sugar a week, which is about the same as four litres of soft drink. Now that was a scary realisation, enough to make me cut back my coffee and tea intake dramatically.

Try this exercise yourself. Write down everything that goes into your mouth—the good, the bad and the ugly. Be honest; after all, no one needs to look at your diary except you. In addition to this, you might find it helpful to also write down what was going on during the day. This may provide some insights into when you eat, what you eat and why.

On particularly stressful days do you tend to go for chocolate? Or do you stop eating altogether? Do you drink more coffee on a Monday morning to get you going for the week? Try to find a relationship between your stress levels and the types of food you eat when you are stressed.

Once you know your eating habits it becomes much easier to start changing them. But until then most observations are only 'guesstimates', often with a conveniently distorted view.

What can I do today?

Start a food diary. Use an exercise book or notepad and carry it with you. It is really important to be 100 per cent honest; you don't need to show it to anyone else, so you'll only be fooling yourself if you 'forget' to record the chocolate bar or round of seconds at lunchtime. This is simply a tool to help you identify your negative eating habits and how they relate to your stress levels. Once you know where you are going wrong you can start to do something about fixing it.

#62 Alcohol, coffee, nicotine, sugar . . . what's your drug of choice?

If you're anything like me, when you get run-down, under pressure or out of control you reach for your own particular poison, or combination of poisons. For most people these are alcohol, caffeine, nicotine and sugar. Personally I have used all four with dazzling effect at various stages in my life.

It's easy to justify that takeaway coffee to get the brain going, a few drinks after work to relax, a sugar fix for that afternoon energy boost or a quiet cigarette break to get out of the office. But the more stressed and overwhelmed you get, the more you rely on these chemicals to get you through your day.

I'm not going to demand you go cold turkey, after all that is up to you; but I do suggest that you get to know your 'poison'. Mine is coffee—I used to drink about 20 cups a day (and sleep like a baby). That was a long time ago, at a stage in my life when I was utterly overwhelmed by my business. I didn't realise what a crutch coffee had become; also, for some reason it liked to hang out with its brothers, alcohol, nicotine and sugar, so before long I was using them all just to get through the day. Coffee and nicotine in the morning, sugar in the afternoon and alcohol at night—and I was only 18 at the time.

Today my only vice is coffee, but I now limit myself to three cups per day (to some people that would still be a lot). It is a battle and I have to be ever-diligent, because the more stressed and under pressure I am the more I crave caffeine and the rest. I also know how terrible I feel if I relent and dose up on coffee and sugar. My brain goes all foggy, I get nervy and jittery and I usually get a headache. Just the way you want to feel when a hundred people are clamouring for your attention.

I have a number of friends who drink a bottle of wine every night, 'to help them relax'. When does it become a crutch or an addiction? It is a thin line, one that I know many of us have walked along. Be honest with yourself and be clear on the benefits of being healthier; the lifestyle changes will soon follow.

What can I do today?

What is your poison? Identify it and think about the benefits of either cutting it out of your diet or reducing it. If you are concerned that it is a more serious problem, get help. There are many places to find help; start with your doctor.

#63 What exactly does eating well mean?

Today, most of us think we have a pretty good idea about which foods are good for us and which aren't. There are literally thousands of books and websites available on this topic; however, much of the information is conflicting, which certainly makes deciding what is good for you more than a little confusing.

To illustrate this point, at certain times in my life I have been advised, either by teachers, doctors or through the media, to avoid the following: eggs, potatoes, red meat, oils, dairy products, nuts, bread, breakfast cereal, tea and red wine. At other times I have been advised to make sure I eat the following: eggs, potatoes, red meat, oils, dairy products, nuts, bread, breakfast cereal, tea and red wine.

When it comes to food, I think people have to make up their own mind which 'food philosophy' they are going to follow. I came up with my own food philosophy simply because I got sick and tired of all the conflicting information.

My food philosophy is:

- Try to eat organic food wherever possible.
- Shop around the outside of the grocery store (i.e. in the fruit and vegetable section, meat, grain and fresh foods).
- Avoid processed foods as much as possible.
- Avoid sugar (especially hidden sugars).
- Read the labels of the food I buy.
- Everything in moderation.

There is a powerful link between eating well and performing well. If your body is functioning well, you will be better able to deal with stress and the pressures of running a business and having a life. To some people this tip will seem so blatantly obvious as to be absurd. Yet unfortunately, for many people, health falls low on the totem pole in a world full of pressure and demands.

I have a good friend, Paul Hockey, who is a one-armed mountain climber. He was recently the first disabled person to climb the face of Mount Everest, and I asked him what he ate when it came to training for major climbs. His advice was simple—eat lots of fresh fruit, vegetables and meat, and avoid processed foods and chemicals.

There are so many sources of information when it comes to deciding what to put into your body. The best tool you can use to decide what is good for you is education. Learn about the different foods, but read widely and don't just accept the first thing you read in a book or on the internet. Check the source—is it credible and knowledgeable? Talk to other people who are healthy and informed. Ask your doctor and other health professionals for their opinions. But most importantly, collect as much information as you can and make informed decisions on your own health and wellbeing.

One of the best ways to restore balance and harmony to your life is to eat well and have a healthy, well-fuelled body.

What can I do today?

Do you have a 'food philosophy'? If not, why not create one today? If you aren't sure where to start, you can visit a dietician or explore an independent or government-funded nutritional website.

#64 Learn to enjoy food again

One of the biggest challenges I face in relation to food is finding the time to eat it. This sounds silly, but in the heat of the work day, with phones ringing, meeting after meeting and people lining up outside my door with various issues to be dealt with, it really is easy to simply bypass eating until later in the day.

That is exactly what I did for many years. I would eat very little during the day, and then I would go home and gulp down a huge, rich meal at around 8 p.m., convincing myself that it was OK because I hadn't eaten much during the day. The rest of the day I lived on coffee and sugary treats to keep my energy up.

Now I know how unhealthy that was and what a strain it was on my body. During a six-year period of eating like this I put on about 40 kilograms.

Through a very necessary and heartfelt desire to lose weight I started to read more about healthy eating and realised that I was doing it all wrong. The three main areas where I was getting it wrong were:

1. I never ate breakfast.
2. I ate big meals at night.
3. I ate really fast.

All of the above made me realise that eating was a chore, not a joy, for me. I didn't see meals as an opportunity for social interaction or to stop and take a breath; rather, eating was something I was doing just to stay alive.

So I had to reassess the way I ate and retrain myself. Yes, I started eating breakfast, but I will talk about that in the next tip. But the biggest thing I did was to start to enjoy eating again, to look forward to it and to take the time to savour it rather than gulp it down.

Today, eating is a joy rather than a chore. I eat out for lunch just about every day, and I look at this as an opportunity to eat a good meal and spend time with friends, clients or work colleagues. It is a break in the day, it is fun and I eat in restaurants where I know I can get a healthy meal.

However, in really busy times I find myself sliding back into the old habit of missing meals, and I have to stop and read myself the riot act. No matter how busy my day is, I know that I need to take a break and enjoy the food in front of me. Then I can get back into it with all the more energy and enthusiasm for having had a good meal.

If this tip strikes a chord with you, don't worry, you are not alone. It surprises me how many business owners put themselves last in all that they do. They pay themselves last, they feed themselves last, they leave the office last. It is time to start putting yourself first!

What can I do today?

If you rarely stop to eat a meal, make next week the one in which you break this habit. Stop for lunch every day. Make it a social occasion: meet some friends out for lunch or invite them in. Allocate at least an hour to have a good lunch, and enjoy every minute. When you get back to work, take a moment to see how you feel.

#65 Get your day off to a healthy start

I didn't eat breakfast for 35 years. Several coffees was all I needed to get my engine going in the morning. My excuse was either that I didn't have enough time or that I was never hungry. Then, a few years back, in a desire to get fit and live past my 40th birthday, I took on a couple of delightful personal trainers. To say that they were appalled by my eating habits was an understatement. While I actually ate good food on the whole, the problem was *when* I ate. As mentioned in the previous tip, eating was a chore, done once a day, late at night. The very worst way to eat.

Sam and Kelly gave me the following guidelines: eat like a king in the morning, like a prince during the day and like a pauper at night. This is probably the best advice I have ever received when it comes to healthy eating.

To kickstart my new eating plan, they told me to eat whatever I liked for breakfast. They didn't care if I had bacon and eggs every day as long as I ate breakfast. Once they had changed my eating habits they could then fix up my diet.

So I started eating breakfast. Now I have it every single day. I don't always have bacon and eggs, but I make a point of eating something even when I am not hungry. It has taken quite some time to get the hang of it, but now I really look forward to having breakfast. What I notice most is that my brain works better, I am definitely calmer and feel I can cope better with the day ahead. I no longer live on nervous energy.

When possible I make breakfast a social experience as well. I live in Cairns, tropical North Queensland, where it is warm all year round. So meeting for breakfast is easy as people tend to be early risers. I have several breakfast meetings each week and I really enjoy them.

If you don't eat breakfast, changing this habit will play a key role in restoring balance and harmony to your life. Your body wants food in the morning; you simply need to start listening to it.

What can I do today?

Commit to eating breakfast every day of the year. It doesn't matter what you start with; once you get into the habit of having breakfast every day, you can then work on changing what it is you eat. But first things first for those non-breakfast eaters.

#66 Water water everywhere

When we get stressed, overtired and overwhelmed we often turn to stimulants to get us through. Unfortunately this can become habit-forming, and it is easy to become dependent on things like sugar and caffeine for that little 'pick me up' during the day.

What you really need, though, is more water in your system. Drinking water is calming and relaxing. Some experts suggest that we should drink up to two litres of water every day. The most important consideration is having plenty of water available so that it is easier to grab a glass of water than a sugary or caffeine-rich alternative.

Today I have two water coolers in my business (for about ten people), and I am thinking about getting another one in my own office. Having access to high-quality, filtered water should, in my opinion, be a basic requirement in every workplace.

As for filtered water versus tap water, personally, I think that unless you know exactly what is in the tap water (or what isn't in it) stick with filtered. Also, remember it isn't just the water but how it gets to you. Are the pipes healthy? How often is the water tested where it comes out from your tap (I bet never)? But as discussed earlier, don't take my word for it—do your own research and form your own opinion. There has been some amazing work done on researching water quality and the filtered-versus-tap-water debate.

When water is readily available you are more likely to drink more of it. Here are some ways to incorporate more water into your life:

• Start your day with two glasses of water, ideally with a couple of squirts of fresh lemon juice. This is a great way to start the day and cleanse your system.
• Get into the habit of always ordering water with your meal, your coffee or your alcoholic drink.

- Keep a jug of water on your desk. Fill it up every morning with fresh water and aim to drink around two litres a day.
- Carry a bottle of water with you wherever you go. This becomes habit-forming after a while. Keep some bottles ready to go in the refrigerator so that you can grab them and run.

The more water you have in your life the better. A water cooler is a cheap item and one that every business should have.

What can I do today?

Do you drink enough water? Why not try at least one of the suggestions in this tip for the next week and see whether it makes a difference to the way you feel. If you don't have a water cooler in your business, grab the Yellow Pages or go online and organise one. It is a tax deduction and will only be beneficial to your business.

#67 Eating out doesn't need to be unhealthy

Eating out can cause the best laid plans to come undone. This can be a real problem for people who have to entertain clients a lot. In fact, most people tend to eat out more often now than ever before, and I recommend it as a great way to reduce stress and get you out of your workplace to clear your head. So we could all use a few tips to make the experience a healthier one. Try the following tips—they work for me:

- Some restaurants are simply better than others when it comes to healthy food choices. Try to select a restaurant that you know has healthy options. Be open with the people you are dining with and let them know why you want to eat in a particular restaurant.
- Think about the type of food you want to eat before you get to the restaurant. Visualise it and set your mind on it rather than arriving there not really knowing what you want.
- Take your time reading the menu. Don't just pick something because it's easy and you are feeling pressured.
- Avoid menu items that have rich or creamy sauces, or are deep-fried.
- Don't be afraid to ask questions about the menu; there are always alternatives. For example, ask for salad dressing on the side or steamed vegetables instead of chips.
- Ask the waiting staff for healthy recommendations. Get to know the staff at the restaurants where you go regularly. They are more likely to go the extra mile if you remember their names and are polite and friendly. Tell them that you are on a health kick and ask for their help. You will be surprised at how supportive they will be.
- Most restaurants are happy to make you a healthy meal if you ask them. If you are worried about ordering something that is healthy but might take a long time to prepare, ask the staff to rush the order through.

- Avoid incidentals such as soft drinks, alcohol, desserts, breads and rich foods. Take these five things off the menu and you can dine out just about anywhere and still leave feeling healthy.

What can I do today?

Next time you are faced with dining out, re-read this tip. Instead of dreading the experience you will soon be able to embrace restaurant dining, enjoy it fully and not have that overpowering sense of guilt with each mouthful.

#68 Encourage healthy eating in your workplace

In an attempt to do a good deed I once let a local charity put a chocolate box in my reception. I am sure you know the ones: you pay a couple of dollars and in return you get a handful of chocolates. A nice concept until everyone in the office starts putting on weight, getting pimples and falling prey to mood swings.

I had to ask the charity to remove the box; I would gladly give them a weekly donation if I could do it without getting the sugar in return. This exercise made me realise the duty of care we have as small business owners when it comes to encouraging healthy eating habits in our workplace. Of course, you can't dictate what people eat, but you can ensure healthy options are available.

A few years ago I tried to put this into practice by purchasing a box of organic fruit once a week for everyone in the office. Unfortunately, after about two months I stopped doing this because most of the time I threw the fruit away, which was a real waste. Having said that, I think we have all become much more health conscious more recently and it is probably a good time to try this exercise again.

There are lots of ways to encourage healthy eating in your workplace. One really good way that I have seen work in a number of businesses is a healthy-eating noticeboard with takeaway menus and phone numbers of healthy-eating options located close by the business. Members of staff who have an interest in healthy eating update the board and ensure that the information is current and accurate.

In the office, providing alternatives to caffeine, low-fat milk and sugar substitutes all help to encourage healthy lifestyles. If there are only sugary, caffeinated options around, that's what people will drink. As mentioned in tip #66, ensuring that there is an abundance of cool, filtered water available really does go a long way to providing an alternative to soft drinks.

Encouraging without dictating is key here. I recently visited one business where coffee wasn't 'allowed' on the premises, and neither were soft drinks, chocolate or any other junk foods. I don't think that being a dictator on what people can and can't eat is the right way to go about it. It is just like the old adage, you can lead a horse to water but you can't make it drink. If someone told me what I could or couldn't eat or drink at work I would tell them a thing or two in return.

So let people make their own decisions about what they want to eat or drink. The best way to encourage healthy eating is to lead by example. From my experience the more healthy the boss is the more healthy the rest of the staff tend to be.

While it is really important to be aware of what you are eating, it is also very important to think about when and where you eat. Whenever I go into a workplace where everyone is eating at their desk as they work, gulping down whatever they can get their hands on, I get a real sense of things being out of balance. As business owners we should provide a calm, clean and relaxed environment for people to eat, and we should ensure that staff take the time to stop and enjoy their meal. Just as stress and pressure spread like fire, so does calm and control. If you are trying to be more balanced, focused and peaceful, yet everyone around you is freaking out because they are overworked, tired and unhealthy, you are fighting a big battle and one that I don't think you can win.

To be cool, calm and collected you need all those around you to be the same. Be proactive and create a healthy work environment; you will be amazed at what a difference this will make. As a delightful by-product, your business will also run more smoothly and be more successful.

What can I do today?

Has your business become a junk-food haven? Are soft drink and chocolate available but nothing else? Well, today you can change that by introducing some alternatives. Put up a 'healthy-eating' noticeboard, get the local greengrocer to deliver a box of fruit once a week, or buy some caffeine alternatives.

#69 When it comes to food, always be prepared

One of my excuses for not eating well was that I never had any healthy food in the cupboard. I dreaded going to the super-market and dealing with the crowds, the hassle and the decisions that had to be made (pathetic, really, I know). Once again, with the help of my long-suffering personal trainers, I retrained my underdeveloped shopping skills and turned what was once a chore into something I now really enjoy.

They helped me to realise that if I didn't have food at home I was likely to buy takeaways on the way home, and that gener-ally this would be something hot and fast and not that healthy. So I learned to plan ahead and drop into the supermarket most days on the way home from work. In addition, I started to visit the local fresh produce market, where all of the really good foods can be found. By this I mean the freshest of fruits and vegetables, the best cuts of meat, seafood straight from the ocean—not frozen—and so on. After a short time both of these activities actually became quite enjoyable. I got to know the store owners and stallholders and other customers, and slowly but surely my shopping trips became social outings.

Spend enough time at the produce markets and you soon get to know the growers personally and discover who sells the best fruit and vegetables. It can also become quite social and a nice way to while away an hour or two on a Saturday morning.

Changing my shopping patterns has meant that I now usually have a good range and stock of fresh fruit and veg-etables in my apartment. This forms a good basis to make plenty of healthy meals and to avoid snacking on junk.

I learned that the key for me was planning ahead, some-thing I am sure that many of you would simply take for granted. Now, in the morning I think about what my day has in store—if I know I am going out for lunch I will plan to have a light meal in the evening, and make a mental note of what I have available and what I need to buy.

To make it even easier to plan healthy meals I started a recipe book that I keep in the car. Now I can flick through my favourite meals and decide what to buy before I head into the supermarket. I go in with a mission and I can be in and out as fast or as slow as I like. Beats standing in the aisles, ravenous but without a clue what to buy.

I know that the few minutes I spend each day actually planning what to eat and when has really helped me to be more aware of what I put into my mouth, in turn making me a much healthier and more relaxed person. Sure, I don't get it right all the time and I have a few more kilograms to budge, but every year I feel healthier than the year before, and that means I am winning the battle.

What can I do today?

Start planning your food intake for the day. Make sure you are organised so you don't find yourself scratching your head wondering what to eat and then grabbing a takeaway.

#70 The 80 per cent rule—let your hair down from time to time

In this section I've described some of the practical steps and helpful tips that really helped me to adopt a healthier lifestyle. Now let's do a bit of a reality check. If I said that you could never eat a chocolate bar again you'd probably give up on healthy eating altogether. Let's be realistic: some days you will just let go of caution and eat what you feel like, even if it isn't completely healthy. And sometimes you will want to reward yourself for all the hard work you put into your life and your business.

The trick is to ensure that you have a far greater number of healthy days than unhealthy days. If eating healthily all the time just gets too hard, aim to eat well *most* of the time. The trick is moderation; drinking alcohol to excess is not good for any of us, but it sure is nice to have a glass of red wine with dinner or an icy cold beer on a hot day. Total abstinence rarely works for a long or sustainable period of time.

A healthy lifestyle isn't like being in a schoolyard or a maximum-security prison where you are told what to do and when to do it. Being healthy is a choice—*your* choice. As we get older we start to realise how important it is. The effects of age and stress start to take their toll; the odd illness and repetitive aches and pains confront us with the realisation that we are getting older and our bodies will not last forever. This is when many people find the motivation to stop smoking or start exercising (and try to fit into a pair of ten-year-old shorts that, sadly, will never ever fit us again).

I am a big believer in moderation. Spend more time being healthy than being unhealthy, put more good things into your body than bad things and you are well on the way to being healthier.

What can I do today?

On the following page write down which of these tips you are going to act on today. A healthy lifestyle shouldn't stop you enjoying life—it will simply make you better able to cope with the challenges life throws at you. Aim to live healthily at least 80 per cent of the time and you will be well on the way to a much more balanced and harmonious life.

Action page—What I need to do to regain balance in my life

----

9 | Invite balance into your workplace

One look around the average workplace and it's easy to spot the presence of an out-of-balance business owner. There are piles of files and papers everywhere, old magazines, stressed-out staff, an obvious lack of attention to details, and much more. To create a balanced workplace is an important and very conscious decision. Start with the way you deal with your day-to-day business activities and your attitude towards them.

The tips in this section will give you some very practical ways to make balance at work the norm rather than the exception. That said, breaking those nasty old habits is always a challenge and may require radical changes to the way you currently do things. If what you are doing is not working, change it, finish it, clean it up.

#71 Get rid of unfinished business
#72 Make the hard decisions—stop procrastinating
#73 Encourage change and reward everyone who embraces it
#74 Some things can never be measured in dollars and cents
#75 Reschedule your day to suit you and the way you like
     to work
#76 Schedule time for interaction/relaxation and just thinking
#77 Outsource/delegate the jobs you really don't like doing
     (and probably do poorly anyway)

#71 Get rid of unfinished business

One of the biggest causes of stress in my life is that never-ending list of unfinished business. This includes unfinished projects, personal things that I never seem to find the time to do, complicated problems—either personal or professional—that are just plain difficult to sort out, fixing things that keep falling off (in my case, door handles around my apartment), and trying to catch up with the people I haven't managed to connect with. I used to have a pile on my desk which was virtually nothing but unfinished business, and once in a while I would shuffle through the mess but I wouldn't really achieve anything.

About two years ago I decided that I had had enough of this pile, which seemed to mock me every time I looked at it. I realised that, to get it sorted once and for all, I had to give it some attention—so I did.

I got a notepad and started to work through that pile. I made up a very comprehensive list of unfinished business items and what I needed to do to get every single item off the list.

The prospect was daunting, but I set a four-week time frame and made a commitment to myself to completely clear my unfinished business list—and I did. And it felt fantastic. The relief was amazing. Emboldened by my success, I applied the technique to the other piles in my life. I highly recommend trying this for yourself.

Today I still have an unfinished business pile on my desk, but it is much smaller and I make a point of not letting it get away from me. I allocate time each week to unfinished business. Most of the items in the pile really just need me to sit and focus for a few minutes on how best to handle them, and think about who else I might possibly need to get involved to help.

What can I do today?

Go through your unfinished business pile and make a list of what you need to do to get every single item off your desk. Set yourself a time frame and start working your way through the list.

#72 Make the hard decisions — stop procrastinating

Procrastination is another common cause (and effect) of being out of balance or overwhelmed in your business. Some decisions are just plain hard—especially the big ones like sacking a staff member, trying to placate an unhappy client or making a major equipment purchase. Often we need to work ourselves into the right frame of mind to make a big decision, and we know that knee-jerk reactions are not a good idea.

The typical cycle that becomes self-perpetuating is that the longer we delay the decision-making process, the more decisions need to be made. Then we start to feel a little overwhelmed and, in struggling to find the time or the energy to make the right decision in the right manner, we procrastinate further and even more decisions then need to be made.

I try to set time frames around my decision-making processes. Let's say I have to decide if I want to work on a specific project or venture that someone has offered me. I make a point of telling the person on the spot how long I need to make my decision, and then set my mental time frame and write it in my diary (AG must respond to Bill Smith by Thursday 10 a.m.). So then it is in my mind and in my diary, and I have to make the decision on time. It normally works; if the deadline arrives and I am still undecided I tend to say no, as I believe that if it is that hard to decide then I shouldn't really do it.

The process is really no different when you have to make hard decisions such as whether to terminate a non-performing member of staff. Set a time frame, spend some time in the build-up to the deadline to make sure you know how you will handle the situation, and then stick to your decision.

It is amazing how your mind gets accustomed to making decisions once you get the decision-making process moving again. The worst place to be is in the non-decision-making mode because issues back up, you get more stressed and overwhelmed and the cycle continues.

What can I do today?

Start setting timelines for your decision-making processes. You have to get decisions flowing no matter how hard it feels. The fewer decisions you make the more back-up there will be, and the more pressured and overwhelmed you will feel.

#73 Encourage change and reward everyone who embraces it

Constant change is a given in the modern business world. Everything changes—all the time, and at a fast and furious pace. The ways that I communicate, travel, manage, market and run my business are completely different today to what they were, say, five years ago, and I can only imagine what things will be like in another five years. Mamma mia!

There are two types of people, in my mind. The first are those who love change and really embrace it. They thrive on it, they are up to speed with technology or at least willing to try it, and they are open and flexible to new ideas and better ways of doing business. Then there are those who simply can't stand change. The mere mention of the word is enough to make them break into a cold sweat, and trying to introduce them to new ideas is like pulling teeth.

So how does this affect you and your business–life balance? This question is best answered by my own story. As mentioned earlier, my business looks and feels very different today to what it did five years ago. It is dynamic, evolving and technologically dependent. We have clients throughout Australia, I travel a lot, I meet a lot of people and have countless opportunities and projects sent my way. We need to constantly adapt to changing markets, new opportunities and new work practices. If my team were not proactive with this I could not do what I do. At times I drive them crazy with changes of direction and demands to always be striving to do what we do better than anyone else, to embrace technology and offer new products and services.

Luckily for me, most of them can cope, although occasionally as I look around the boardroom table I can almost hear them thinking, 'Not more change!' But to their great credit they support me 100 per cent and help me to achieve my goals and objectives. Best of all, they have a 'can do' attitude.

In return, I realise that I have to restrain myself a little at times and not overwhelm them with too much change too fast. Over the years not everyone has been able to cope, and I have had a few people resign simply because the pace of the business was too fast, with too much change to suit them; I admire them for admitting it and moving on.

My message is that change is here to stay. Some people simply don't seem to be able to 'do' change. The best advice I can offer is to enter into open and honest dialogue about change and what it means to you. Try to nurture people through it or at least provide an environment where it can be discussed. If necessary, get professional help. There are people who are experts at change management and they can be very valuable when dealing with organisational changes at every level.

What can I do today?

Decide what your philosophy is towards change and what it means to you. Take a few moments to write it down, then sleep on it. Once you're happy with it, put it in a place where you can see it often and your staff can see it, too. Introduce the concept of change and start to gauge people's feelings about it.

#74 Some things can never be measured in dollars and cents

All too often business success or failure is measured purely in terms of dollars and cents. I find this approach really wrong; a change in headspace is needed. In dealing with literally thousands of business owners around the world, either through my books or through seminars, most of them seem caught up on the same issue. They overlook their other successes and evaluate what they do based on what kind of car they drive or the size of their house.

I love small business and everything that it stands for. It represents people willing to give life a go, to go out on a limb and be brave enough to take a risk and put everything on the line. But most of all I love the fact that most small businesses are actually very good at what they do—and this is because of that vested interest and risk. They know that losing a customer will have a very direct effect on their personal income.

If a person working for a large organisation loses a customer it is unlikely to cost them anything personally (unless it is a very big customer); their income is reasonably secure regardless of the outcome of the situation.

This said, though, to me the real success of small businesses is what their owners build and achieve. I encounter truly amazing people doing amazing things, often for marginal profit or sometimes none at all. But they are proud of what they do, the service they provide, the jobs they create and the reputation they are building.

But many of us need to stop and take stock more often. Rather than just looking at how much money is in the bank at the end of the week, we should post a victory board highlighting the successes we have had that week as well. What great things did we achieve?

Changing the way we think about success makes us more forgiving and understanding of ourselves. We start to say things like, 'I haven't got a lot of money in the bank, but I do have a lot of very happy customers. The money will come.' And believe me, it does.

What can I do today?

Set up your own victory board. Make sure that every achievement in your business is noted, for they are all relevant. It could be a new customer, a sales record, an award, a letter from a happy customer or supplier, an industry acknowledgment, a milestone like the business's first birthday, and so on. It will change the way you think about your business and the way you measure success. It will raise your morale and that of your staff.

#75 Reschedule your day to suit you and the way you like to work

Often we end up working within a schedule that suits everyone else but ourselves. It doesn't have to be that way. Some people work better in the morning than in the afternoon, while others are the opposite. Some people like to exercise in the middle of the day and flourish with a couple of hours to go to the gym. The key here is that it is better to work in the manner that suits you than try to fit your life in around your work. Often all it takes is a change in mindset.

Many of my clients plan their trading hours and the days they work around their lifestyle. It is very empowering to do this. The counterargument for many people is that they have to be open for their customers—and yes, this is very relevant for some businesses, but not for all. And even if your business has to be open at certain hours, do you have to be there at those times?

A big part of this tip is about letting go of perceptions. Many business owners live in a state of near terror over changing anything to do with their customers. They don't want to change the business name or the logo or the brand, or the hours the business is open, or the products or services being offered. But while I am an advocate of consistency when it comes to delivering a product or service, customers are much more open to change than most business owners think. In fact, they like it—because it shows that the business is getting better.

Think about it for a moment. If you are working like a dog and you're exhausted, lacking in enthusiasm and not really having a jolly time, do you think that your customers can't see or feel this? If you change the way you work so that it suits your lifestyle and needs better, you will be much more energetic and engaging at work, and your customers will get a far better level of service and a more enjoyable experience. You simply need to be brave enough to do it.

The first step in the process is analysing how you actually like to work. If you aren't a morning person (whatever that means), then arrange your business so you don't have to be there in the morning. If you find it hard to get anything done at work because you are constantly being distracted by the demands of staff, suppliers and others, work from home one day each week and give clear instructions on who can contact you and for what. I have found I get more done in one day at home than I do for the rest of the week at work. It is amazing.

The traditional way of doing business is often not applicable in the modern world. Set up your business to suit you. If you are reading this book in anticipation of going into business for yourself, think about this long and hard before you make your move. Buy or start a business that suits the way *you* want to live. If you are a night person don't buy a milk run. If you are a recovering alcoholic it probably isn't a good idea to buy a nightclub. If you are afraid of sharks don't become a commercial diver. You get the drift, as silly as my examples might be. Make your business work for you, rather than you work for it.

What can I do today?

What one simple change can you introduce to your business today that will make it suit your lifestyle better than it does now? Implement this change—tell your staff, tell your customers, tell anyone you want to, but make the change.

#76 Schedule time for interaction/relaxation and just thinking

It took a good friend to give me a little guidance on this topic. A few years ago my typical work practice was to get to the office at around 6.30 every morning. I would then set about making my 'to do' list for the day, which typically had about a million items on it in my attempt to do as much as I possibly could. Of course, it would be impossible to get everything done on the list in a month, let alone a week, but I didn't know any better.

One day I was having a coffee with this friend and I happened to jot down a few things in my notebook. She saw my 'to do' list and, with a look of shock, she asked, 'When do you find time to just sit and think?' Now, that was a powerful question because I didn't allow any time for that. In fact, from the minute I got to work to the minute I left I pretty well ran all day, often not even bothering to stop and eat, fuelled only by coffee (with sugar).

From that day on I made a point of putting aside some time each day to do nothing but think and reflect. Sometimes I might allocate 30 minutes; if I have a lot on my mind I might allocate an entire morning. I also give myself 30 minutes every morning to walk around the office, say hello to everyone and just connect with my team. What is going on, who is doing what, are there any pressing issues that need my attention, and so on.

I am amazed at how empowering this feels and how it has reduced my stress and the feeling of being overwhelmed. Our brains need time to process information, and the more information coming in the more time they need to process it. If you don't give your brain time to work through things it keeps them in a holding pattern, with more items being added every day.

Give yourself some quiet time to simply think things through. Don't try to fill every minute of every day. Make the time to connect with those around you. There are so many benefits in doing this, not the least of which will be a feeling of control and calmness instead of feeling thrown into the fray every time you walk through the door.

What can I do today?

Look at your daily schedule and allocate some time to just sit and think. It might not be practical to do this at your workplace. Maybe on the way to work you can stop at a park or a coffee shop, or maybe do it on the way home. It's up to you to figure out what works for you, but learn to look at this time as a real investment in you and your business.

#77 Outsource/delegate the jobs you really don't like doing (and probably do poorly anyway)

As a marketing consultant I encounter a lot of people at their wit's end with marketing. They know they have to do it, but they don't know how or what to do so it becomes an irritation rather than an opportunity. There are many facets to running a business that we don't like and that generally we are not very good at.

In my business I am the ideas man. I love coming up with new ways to do what we do, to develop creative concepts for my clients, to write books, to give keynote presentations and to train people. But give me a profit and loss statement or an operations manual and I have the attention span of a flea.

Several years ago I realised that my business was getting a little out of control. I made up a list of all the general groups of tasks that needed to be done, who was doing what and, overall, how well were they being managed. It became glaringly obvious that the jobs people didn't like doing were all being done badly. So the first step was to work out which particular tasks people in my team did like doing. From here we matched up the tasks with the people, as much as we could. The tasks that nobody liked to do or that could not be done effectively needed to be outsourced rather than mismanaged.

In the end we outsourced all our computer maintenance, bookkeeping, artwork, customer service follow-up, and buying flowers for the office—an eclectic list, but it worked very well for us. Now all of the above are managed magnificently by service providers, instead of having me or one of the team bumble through something that we are not good at or don't like. And if you ask me, the cost of most of these tasks has been reduced by having an expert do them, and freeing my staff's time and energy to focus on what they're good at—delivering quality work and making money for the business.

Getting rid of those jobs that drive you crazy is normally much easier and less expensive than you think. If you are unconvinced, pick just one and start there.

What can I do today?

Make up a list of the tasks that you really don't like doing (and, if you are honest, which you know you do poorly). Pick one that you can outsource to someone else so that you never have to think about it again. It is incredibly liberating and stress-relieving. Give it a try.

Action page—What I need to do to regain balance in my life

----

10 | Balancing the business and the family

Trying to balance a business and a life is challenging. Add a family to the equation and things get even tougher. We know that family should come first, but for some reason they often get overlooked by the most demanding child of all—a small business.

Throughout this book I encourage you to question what you are doing in your life now and seek to understand why you are so out of balance. The road to taking control will then be much clearer and the end goal certainly more achievable. Most of the tips in this book apply equally to people with or without families. This section is for the business owner who also has a family.

This section will also be useful for anyone considering starting a family or a business, and thinking about how you will juggle the two. It may save you some heartache down the line.

#78   What is your family plan and how does it work with your business?
#79   Change your business to suit your family
#80   Does your business suit your family?
#81   Remember the oxygen mask
#82   Applying lessons from family life to your business
#83   Family fun and fitness
#84   Save some energy for the good times
#85   Clearly define the boundaries between the family and the business
#86   Give your kids some great memories

#78 What is your family plan and how does it work with your business?

Just as we should have clear goals for our businesses, it's equally important to have a sense of direction and clarity about where you and your family are heading. I recommend developing a family plan.

People who set goals tend to achieve them. Often just sitting down to talk about the future can be quite an eye-opener. For example, have you ever considered the following questions in relation to you and your family? The questions can be asked of you as an individual and also collectively of the family—an interesting exercise:

1. What do you want out of life—what are your dreams and aspirations?
2. What are your greatest fears?
3. Where do you want to live? Why?
4. How many children do you want to have?
5. What kind of lifestyle do you want to have?
6. What are your concerns for your children?
7. What do you want to provide for them, and in what time frame?
8. What will you need in order to do this?
9. What is most important in your relationship?
10. What are your views on family health and wellbeing?

Some of these are hard questions to answer, and in the midst of a busy life we seldom take the time to sit down and think them through. We just get on with it. But discussing topics like these and then putting in place a simple plan will have enormous benefits for your family life.

So how do you write a family plan? It can be as simple or as complex as you want it to be. For me, a one-page snapshot does it—use the questions above to determine what your goals are, then prioritise, setting realistic time frames and a way to measure when you have achieved your goals. Also, it is important to allocate some personal responsibilities as well.

Reality is the key word here. Sure, we would all like to take the family first class to Disneyland—but if you are struggling to pay the mortgage it is not that likely at this stage. So by all means put it on your list of goals, but make the time frame realistic, otherwise you leave yourself and your family open to disappointment.

As with any long-term plan, it is really important to ensure you achieve some early victories. Say one of your goals is to get the family fitter. Well, starting right now, a daily family walk can be scheduled for after dinner. So you instantly have a goal, with a clear action plan and a time frame. Beautiful.

The next stage is to consider how your family plan fits in with the demands of your business. Can the two work together? Are they in sync, or do one or both need to be modified to fit a little better? Often some small, simple changes can put both the business and the family back on a level and complementary playing field.

One thing I know for certain is that just because you make a family plan doesn't mean there is a guarantee that you and your family will stick to it. Families grow, they evolve, their needs change and so does their focus. Don't be too rigid; understand that your plan gives you a unified approach and some objectives to aim for, but the route you end up taking to achieve these goals may well change.

Many business owners really feel the heat when trying to juggle their family and their business. Being clear on where you and your family are heading will certainly make it less stressful during those times when you need to focus on your business. Even just talking about your family's dreams and aspirations is a step in the right direction.

What can I do today?

Why not sit down with your family tonight and talk about your goals. Where are you going? What do you want to achieve? What do you need to do to help each other get there? Ideally, use this discussion to write up your own family plan.

BALANCING THE BUSINESS AND THE FAMILY

#79 Change your business to suit your family

When one or both parents are involved in running a small business, the family often pays the price. Some people manage both really well, but it isn't always easy.

Family should always come first—we all know this. But in reality they often don't. If you are a business owner who is fighting a battle for balance, something has to give. Unfortunately, those closest to you often get the shortest straw. When there are demands from staff, customers, suppliers and creditors, who all want your attention right now, there isn't a lot of room left for the family.

Perhaps this would be OK if these demands only affected individuals and their families during working hours, but often this pressure spills over into what should be family time. Most small business owners work very long hours to get everything done, and the family tends to come last on the list.

I know many small business owners who have ruined relationships because of their workaholic tendencies, through a misguided sense of responsibility towards their business. In fact, I am one of these people. My ten-year marriage didn't survive my obsession with my business. For some people this is down to pure survival, an attempt to make ends meet. Others have just developed bad habits, thinking it's OK to work ridiculous hours because 'that is what you have to do to make a business work'.

Well, the world is changing, and people are becoming much more flexible and open-minded. The real issue here is making the business work for the family by changing the way you run your business, being less rigid and not just doing things the same way you have always done them.

I actively encourage people to tailor their business to suit them rather than everyone else. Why not set up your business to work the hours that suit you? Why not take your kids to work if you can? If you don't get the chance at any other time, why not take time out in the middle of the day to go the gym? There really is no reason not to make these changes except our own perceptions and limiting beliefs.

There may be a price to pay for this; you might lose the odd customer who doesn't like the fact that you are no longer there at 7 a.m. to answer their questions, but you will gain so much that is priceless. And did you really want that customer in the first place? I once had a client who sacked me because I refused to take his calls at 10 p.m. on a Friday night. Did I want a client that was going to call me on a Friday night after a few glasses of wine, wanting to talk marketing? Certainly not.

It's your business. Tell people why you are making these changes and you may be really surprised to see how supportive they are. More and more people are choosing to run their own businesses, and that means that more families will have small businesses attached to them. Run the business to suit your family rather than the other way around. You will be amazed at how much stress this can remove from your life.

What can I do today?

Can you change the way you run your business to make it more family friendly? Perhaps make little changes to start with. Let people know why you are making these changes and you will generally get their support.

#80 Does your business suit your family?

I am all for people starting their own businesses. If you have a well-established business that can run with less input from you on a day-to-day basis, the freedom of being your own boss can really help on the family front. Perhaps you can be more flexible with your working hours or take the kids to work with you from time to time; and you may make more money working for yourself. At least you know the boss can't complain about you spending time with the family or bringing the kids to work. However, some businesses simply aren't suited to raising a family. Either they take up too much time or keep you busy during the wrong times of the day, or they are simply too demanding and put unreasonable pressure on the owner.

I have met many people who have been happily self-employed and whose only responsibility was to their business. Then they meet someone special, a relationship forms and gets serious, and then a family comes along. All of a sudden the business starts to struggle because the owner isn't able to spend as much time or energy working to build it. As the business limps along finances get tight, stress levels increase, pressure builds and the situation becomes very difficult for all involved, often ending in tears.

Sometimes it is better to work for someone else rather than for yourself. Often it is about timing and what stage you are at in your business and your family. In particular, starting a new business when you have a young family is always going to be challenging. In fact, at any stage of your business's life cycle, if your business and your family are out of alignment or at odds, the chances of having any kind of balance are really quite slim.

If you are currently in the situation where your business responsibilities are clashing with your family life and this is putting great stress and pressure on you, the best answer, as harsh as it may seem, is to change your business. There are always plenty of reasons not to sell your business or even close it down if it is only marginally profitable. However, in this instance selling or closing may ultimately be the most logical decision. It can be quite a relief not to have a business to look after on a daily basis.

What can I do today?

Spend a moment thinking about your business and your family. Does your business complement your family life (or the family life you have planned)? If it does, that's great. But what will you do if it doesn't? Change your business, or change your family?

#81 Remember the oxygen mask

When you watch an aircraft safety demonstration it's a great reminder of the importance of looking after yourself first and foremost. The aircrew or safety video always instructs that parents should put on their own oxygen masks first and then fit masks to their children. It is clearly more important for the parent to be conscious and able to assist the child rather than the other way around. Yet in life, we often forget this very obvious point.

If you are really stressed out, overworked, overwhelmed and making yourself sick in an effort to make your business work, are you really doing the logical thing? Are you making sure that you will be OK so that your family will be OK? Probably not. Running a family and a business is one of the most challenging paths you can take in life, but many people do it successfully.

Self-sacrifice is part of being a parent. It is also generally a part of being a business owner, particularly in the early stages of the business. So if you are sacrificing your own wellbeing in every area of your life, what are you doing for you? The best laid plans can come undone when you form a family and have to consider more people than just yourself. But whether you are single, married, a parent or not, the importance of making sure you are OK first and foremost cannot be overstated.

In fact, your wellbeing becomes all the more important if you have a family. So remember, you have to put on your oxygen mask first to ensure that you are OK and able to help those around you.

What can I do today?

Don't treat yourself differently because you are a parent. The better you feel about your life the better those around you will feel. Adopt the tips in this book regardless of whether you are single or married with a dozen children.

#82 Applying lessons from family life to your business

Running a family and running a business are actually surprisingly similar in many ways. Resolving disputes, crisis management, project management, cash flow, time management—these are all topics that you read about in business books, but you don't often associate them with running a family. Yet these are skills we apply to family life every single day.

Indeed, there's much we can learn from our families that's useful in a business context. For instance, how to deal with people. Children are often the toughest of negotiators, partners the most discerning customers (who may not necessarily be in the market to buy what we are selling), and that's before we get on to the extended family—know-it-all aunties and uncles, cousins, and so on.

We can go one step further and really start to enjoy these observations and perceptions, and learn to appreciate our families more. Sometimes seeing the similarities between our business and our home life introduces perspective, and this somehow makes situations less stressful and an out-of-balance life more manageable.

I guess that the real point I am making here is that you can learn more from your family if you make the time to connect with them. The answer to many of our day-to-day issues could be overcome if we perhaps learned a lesson or two from a five year old. In fact many of the ideas in this book are reflections of what children do—they live in the moment, they love to laugh, they sleep when they need to, they cry when they need to, they eat when they are hungry, and so on. We spend years erasing much of this good internal programming, but now is a good time to start listening to it again. Learn from your family and enjoy the process.

What can I do today?

Identify at least one lesson you learned from your family today and think about how you can apply it to your business. This can be fun and also quite a stimulating challenge. Tell your family about it. Changing your perceptions can often transform a burden into a joy. The difference is what is in our head.

#83 Family fun and fitness

I have spoken about the importance of introducing physical fitness into your life to combat the effects of stress. People often think that having a family will prevent them from finding the time to enjoy a fitness regime. But this doesn't have to be the case. In fact a family can be a very effective reminder of the need to spend time on yourself, recuperating from the pressures of work and enjoying the simple things in life. You don't need to drag the family to the gym or get them to run marathons, but there are many simple activities you can do with your family that are healthy, soothing and restorative.

Something as simple as an after-dinner walk with the kids (with bikes, prams, roller blades, dogs, dolls, etc.) is relaxing, peaceful and really enjoyable. Everyone gets to walk off dinner, burn up some excess energy and talk, play or recharge.

A friend of mine who owns two businesses takes her daughter to swimming lessons every week. While her daughter is learning to swim my friend does laps. She loves it. Weekend picnics, walks in the park, a day at the beach and a host of other activities that all involve fresh air, physical activity and quality family time will benefit every member of the family. It's also really nice to get your head out of your business for a while and think about something else. Exercise, fresh air and family have a wonderful ability to help clear the head and give you a sense of contentment.

So rather than looking at your family as a hindrance to getting fit, look for ways to enjoy being together, relax and get some exercise at the same time. For extra ideas, do an online search for family fitness.

The more you do to bring every part of your life into balance, the better off you will be. By focusing some attention on family fitness you get to enjoy the benefits in every part of your life. You benefit personally, your family benefits and your business will ultimately benefit, too. Now that is a wonderful win–win situation all round.

What can I do today?

Spend an hour online to come up with a list of ways you and your family could spend more time together getting fresh air and being active. Put this list on the wall somewhere where you can all see it. Maybe take it in turns to choose which activity you will do each day or each week.

#84 Save some energy for the good times

It's hard to come home after a long and crazy day, when you've been pulled in a thousand different directions, and be ready to give some quality time to the family. You know you should be saving some of your energy for your family. And you know that the issues you did battle with today will in all likelihood still be there tomorrow, and the day after. But every day that goes by, your children are getting a little older, as are your parents and everyone else you care for. Days are going by that you will never get back again. It's enough to stress you out!

If it takes every minute away from your business for you to recharge so that you can go and do battle again, what you are doing is clearly not working. If you spend all of your spare time sleeping or on the couch watching television, your business is taking too much of a toll on you, your body and your family.

The starting point is to get to know your body, and your energy highs and lows. Aim to do the things you really love doing with your family at the times when you have more energy. If you are a morning person, spend some quality time with your family in the morning, rather than running out the door before everyone else is even out of bed.

Remember, it isn't normal to be totally exhausted after a day at work. It is a sign that something is not right. Sure, from time to time we all feel exhausted, but it should be an occasional incident, not an everyday scenario.

This may also be an excellent time to get a check-up. If you always feel down and exhausted there could be a medical reason. It is wise to check all angles; it might take a few goes to find out if there is a problem that is more than just stress and overwork. Doctors say that the number-one reason people visit them is a general feeling of exhaustion. Sound familiar? Well, you can do something about it so that you can really enjoy life a lot more.

During the worst of my workaholic days I found that I had plenty of energy at work, but crashed at home every evening and on weekends. I changed my diet, got moving and reduced the stress in my life, and was amazed at how much energy this gave me. I know now that when I am really stressed, that exhausted feeling comes back and I don't like it.

Logically, it is much nicer to be feeling great when you have time off, rather than feeling like a complete wreck. So apart from putting the tips in this book into action, try to plan your life so that you can spend more positive and energetic time with your family rather than just giving them the leftovers.

What can I do today?

Several times throughout your day, take a moment to measure your energy level. Rate your energy level from one to ten: one is ready to fall asleep, ten is bouncing out of your skin and being ready, willing and able to run a marathon. Get used to measuring your energy level and start to measure where it is at when you are with your family at various times. Do you only spend time with them when you are at level one, or do they get their fair share of level ten? Awareness is the first step in the change process. Desire to change is the second.

#85 Clearly define the boundaries between the family and the business

I am currently writing a book called *101 Tips for Working with Family, Friends and Lovers*. What a topic! Everyone I talk to who either works with or has worked with family, friends or lovers is keen to pass on their experiences and words of wisdom. In each case I find that the challenges of these working conditions are very easy to identify, but the ways to overcome these challenges are not as clear.

There is one recommendation that has everyone in agreement: that is the importance of clearly defining the boundaries between family and business. This recommendation is critical to achieving success in both the business and family arenas, and to having a balanced life.

Many of the tips and recommendations in this section look at ways to help get the business and the family to fit together a little better. That is a very different process to what I am suggesting here. Boundaries are designed to prevent the business from encroaching unreasonably on your family life. They need to be clearly defined, specific and understood.

Here are ten recommendations for ways to define boundaries between your business and your family:

1. Ensure that your staff know what they can call you about at home and what they can't.
2. Be very careful about giving out your mobile number. If you hand it out to everyone, everyone will call at a time that suits them, not when it suits you.
3. Have specific times when you can't talk business and give these times a name: for example, family time, personal time, recharge time—whatever helps you to remember why you need to forget about the business for now.
4. Never, ever discuss the business in bed. Profit and loss statements are not good foreplay.

5. Allocate times to talk business when you need to. For example, sitting around the dinner table is a good time for everyone to talk about their day and your business day is an important part of this. It is important to share all aspects of the business, the trials and the tribulations, but put a time limit on it.

6. Learn how to leave issues at work. By all means talk about issues but don't be consumed by them. It is great to have rituals (like putting all problem issues in a folder and then in a drawer) that introduce a degree of separation from the issue.

7. If you make promises to your family, keep them. It is better to let down a customer than a family member.

8. Don't let the business get in the way of important family events like birthdays, holidays and Christmas.

9. Ensure that your family know what they can do to help you run your business successfully.

10. Always remember that long after your business goes your family will still be there.

By clearly defining the boundaries between your business and your family, you will automatically reduce some of the stress and pressure associated with trying to balance both. Everyone knows where they stand, and that is a good thing.

What can I do today?

Which of the ten suggestions made in this tip could you use today? Which one struck a chord with you? Actioning any of these tips would only take a few minutes. Enlist your family's help to make them work.

#86 Give your kids some great memories

In tip #26 I spoke about the power of creating 'magnificent moments'—those special interactions where you brighten someone's day, show genuine interest in other people and generally create a moment in time that will be remembered fondly by those concerned. This tip is similar, but it deals specifically with giving your children some great memories. All too often children become the small business orphans as Mum or Dad, or both parents, get stuck working long hours, depriving the kids of quality time.

Give your children great memories of the business and your time in it. Make them a part of it. No matter how dull you may think it is for them, they will be impressed because it is connected with you. A friend of mine says her most wonderful childhood memory was making deliveries with her father, who ran a small goods business. She would spend every Saturday making the rounds with her father. The customers would all spoil her, and as she came from a big family it was the only time she got to spend one on one with her father. The idea of sitting in a truck all day sounds pretty boring to an adult, but to a child it was an exciting new world.

Think back to your own childhood. Do you have fond memories of your parents' work or business? These are often the simplest of memories. What did they smell like when they got home from work? What did they bring home? What were the rituals, such as Friday night treats? What was it like to wander around the business when everyone else had gone home?

I remember my nieces coming to my office; they were absolutely in awe of the fact that I had ten computers. They said I must be really rich, which I must say really made me laugh. The look of awe in their eyes was priceless.

Share the victories, go out and celebrate when good things happen and let the kids know why you are celebrating.

Whatever you do, create some wonderful memories for your children, your partner and yourself. What could possibly be more rewarding than this?

What can I do today?

Do your children share in your business in any way? Plan today what you will do to celebrate your next success and how you will share it with your children. Look for other ways to create great memories with your children. You will get as much out of it as they will.

Action page—What I need to do to regain balance in my life

----

11 | Balancing tips specifically for men

When it comes to managing the day-to-day stresses of business and family, men and women tend to cope in different ways. To help account for these differences, I've done a separate section for women who own their own business (Section 12), and this section here is for the fellas.

Obviously I can't talk for the entire male species, but I can say that the tips I present here are based on meeting and talking to many male business owners who have struggled for years to find some kind of business–life balance. I have no doubt that they will strike a chord with many male readers (and a few female readers trying to figure out what makes us men tick).

#87   Do our successes or failures define us as men?
#88   Men die younger than women—why?
#89   The myth of expectation—most of the time we are wrong
#90   The need to be physical to maintain balance
#91   Male bonding—make sure it's supporting you, not holding you back
#92   Never lose sight of what your partner brings to the relationship
#93   Admitting we are out of control means we are weak—wrong
#94   Treat your body as your most important business asset

#87 Do our successes or failures define us as men?

One thing that men are not good at is failure or, as is often the case, the perception of failure. The thought of failing in your own business is a bit like a caveman going out to catch something for dinner and coming home empty-handed. As men we often base our sense of self-worth on our successes or failures.

But as I mentioned earlier, success can be measured in many different ways, with financial success being just one aspect. It is important for a man to see his business from a larger perspective.

So if you are in business and it doesn't work, and the worst thing possible happens—you go broke—think it through to the full outcome. Yes, you will have lost some money—probably a lot. Your pride will be damaged and you may be a little embarrassed. Hopefully your relationships with your family and friends are intact. So what else can you do except get on with life and start again? Get a job, find some way to start another business, go back to school. But whatever you do, you have to pick yourself up, shake the dirt off and get going. How many hugely successful entrepreneurs have gone broke only to bounce back bigger and bolder each time? The difference between them and other less successful people is that they refused to lie down and give up.

What can I do today?

Think about what you have achieved in your life to reach this point. These can be seemingly small things, like getting onto a sporting team at school, through to big achievements such as finding a partner or becoming a father. Every single person on the planet has many, many achievements in their life—remember what some of yours are and be content to know that you are much more than your business.

#88 Men die younger than women — why?

Some may say this is a conspiracy (only joking, ladies), but there is no doubt that it is a reality—on average, men tend to die younger than women. While there are many reasons for this, one of the main reasons is stress and how we deal with it (or rather, we don't). This is not to say that women have any less stress—they certainly don't—but I think they deal with it better than the average man.

Men carry the often self-imposed responsibility of being the provider for their family—a concept that is biologically logical since they are bigger, stronger and better at catching woolly mammoths. With this responsibility comes the associated stress and pressure. One of the worst insults for a man is to be accused of not being able to support his family, and in the backs of our minds this fear often lurks.

So there is a lot of pressure and stress on us to bring home the mammoth. Over a lifetime this takes its toll on the body and ultimately reduces life expectancy. Now there was a time when men used to sit around campfires talking about this kind of stuff (in our own, very indirect way), and that was a mechanism to get the stress out. Now we tend to spend less and less time with our 'campfire' buddies, and business owners often struggle to find the time to even think about getting together in such an environment—which must be one of total trust and openness, something that takes time to develop.

I encounter this issue frequently—men in business who have become socially isolated, who are struggling to find someone to talk to about their issues and challenges. In fact I would rate it as one of the most significant issues facing men in small business today. They carry the stress, the pressure, the burdens and responsibilities themselves. Often they don't want to unload these on their family (after all, for man—the woolly mammoth hunter, the provider—it isn't good to look 'weak').

If we could find other men to talk openly with about the trials and tribulations associated with running our businesses, our overall stress levels would drop dramatically. Why? Because we would be reassured that all the feelings we are experiencing are completely normal, and that everyone else goes through them as well. We would also be able to get advice from other people who had 'been there, done that', reinforcing the old adage that a problem shared is a problem halved.

What can I do today?

As a man, who can you communicate with openly and honestly about the issues you face in your business? Is there someone who always seems to understand, or someone you look up to? Develop this support, be open about it and explain why you are doing it. You will be surprised at how many men will understand exactly what you are talking about and who will leap at the opportunity to get involved, preferably as a group.

#89 The myth of expectation—most of the time we are wrong

This is an interesting point and one that adds significantly to most men's feelings of pressure and being overwhelmed, and to overall stress levels. We believe that other people have enormous expectations of us, but often they don't.

I have spent a lot of my life achieving, perhaps even over-achieving. I am a very driven person. I am not sure if growing up as an orphan had something to do with it—perhaps I was proving to the world that I would amount to something. Interestingly, one of my greatest reasons for achieving was to make my older sister proud of me. So I worked very hard, always striving, always driven, always achieving. Then one day she died, and I was left with a very hollow feeling and a need to find another reason for my drive and ambition.

I soon arrived at the realisation that I needed to do what I did for me. Not to impress others, or to get their approval. I had to do it for my own complete sense of satisfaction. This realisation was very liberating, to say the least. But with it came another—my sister had loved me completely, uncon-ditionally. She would have loved me and been proud of me whether I cleaned toilets for a living or found a cure for cancer. That was what she was like. I was driven because I thought her expectations were for me to succeed—but I was wrong.

One of my clients visited me not long ago. He was running a small business which wasn't going very well. He was really stressed out and sick, struggling, clearly at the end of his tether. I could tell that he really didn't have it in him to keep going; he was totally exhausted. But his reason for struggling on was that he had borrowed $300 000 from his parents to start this business, which was now failing. He believed that his parents could not afford such a big loss, that it would ruin them completely. We set a plan in place to try to rebuild the business, but deep down I didn't think it was possible because he was so burned out and fragile.

A few days later I received a call out of the blue from his father. He wanted to talk to me as he was concerned about his son's wellbeing. The father's side of the story was very different. He didn't care about the money at all. Yes, it was a hit to take, but he would get over it and move on. His only concern was his son's health, but he was afraid to talk to his son in this manner because he didn't want him to feel like a failure.

Now this was exactly what I am talking about in this section. The expectations that the son had were destroying him. What they had here was a communication problem first and foremost; the business problem was secondary. Fortunately, they were able to resolve their misunderstanding. They sold the business, recouped some of the loss and moved on in a much healthier and happier manner.

Don't assume that you know what expectations people have of you. It is much better to talk, to clarify what their expectations are, and then determine whether you can meet them or not. Don't let your perceptions stress you out.

What can I do today?

What drives you? Who are the people you feel have the highest expectations of you? Would you consider talking to them to see if their expectations really are as high as you think?

#90 The need to be physical to maintain balance

For most men there is a need to feel like a man. This tends to involve being masculine, doing masculine things and being appreciated for being masculine. Now, interestingly enough, while we understand the need for women to feel feminine we don't fully understand or appreciate the need for men to feel masculine.

What this means to an individual varies. For some it may be sport, for some it may be hanging out with other men, for some it may be what they read or watch on TV, or their hobbies. For most, though, there is a physical component. Even though there are many men who are not overly physical, they are stimulated by physical encounters. Watching sport, playing action games, seeing action movies or reading action books—each has a strong physical component, and they are generally considered masculine.

In my opinion, most men need this to balance their lives. Again, though, for most small business owners the biggest issue is time or, more importantly, lack of time. What suffers when there isn't enough time? All these activities, which somehow change from being stress-relieving, balancing pastimes to optional activities that will be done if time permits—which, of course, it rarely does as our responsibility list grows.

The end result—men end up out of balance, feeling less of a man and not really knowing why. Clearly this is a big generalisation, but again, from my experience it is very common and a growing problem.

What can I do today?

What do you do to feed your masculine energy? Do you know what makes you feel more of a man? Make a list of these activities—and, most importantly, make the time in your life, no matter how busy you are, to do them. You will feel much more centred, much calmer and somehow more complete. But make sure you explain this concept to your partner so they understand what you are doing and why.

#91 Male bonding — make sure it's supporting you, not holding you back

One thing about men: we like to bond with other men. It's our tribal biology. A group of fellas sitting around the coffee machine (formerly the campfire) will discuss all kinds of things, most largely irrelevant, but socially safe. Instead of talking about being chased by that sabre-toothed tiger ('Boy, was he a big one!'), today we talk about football, cars, fishing. Business is often a hot topic, and it is always good to be able to air your views and concerns regarding your business with the boys. But this is also a tricky scenario.

Not everyone looks at business in the same way. Some men are bitter and twisted about it, perhaps having had a bad experience in the past. Some may work for a boss and feel that what you are doing is so risky that it is crazy. Some may be secretly jealous of you for having a go. And, of course, there will be some who will support you unconditionally because they are loyal and true friends who are proud of what you have achieved.

Whatever the case, it is important for men to be strong enough to know when the other men in their lives are a good influence and when they are not. If you are struggling to find balance between business and home, you want an understanding ear but not a manipulative one. Going out and getting drunk is not going to help matters. Neither will sitting around and bitching about how tough life is.

The point I am trying to make is that while we need our male friends around us, we also need to be able to tell when they are being supportive and when they are being destructive. I am very aware of the negative influence that some men can have. They are so bitter and twisted that they have absolutely nothing positive to say about anything. I don't have room for people like this in my life anymore, and I won't waste my time with them. Sounds harsh, but it is necessary. If you want to succeed in business and have a balanced life, surround yourself with successful, balanced people whom you respect and admire.

What can I do today?

Look around you. Are there any male friends in your life who are bringing you down? It's your choice, but do you really want them affecting you? Maybe reading them the riot act will make them take stock of their own lives and stop being so miserable.

#92 Never lose sight of what your partner brings to the relationship

I often encounter bitter and twisted men who have gone through a divorce and ended up having to buy their spouse out of their business. Many of these men seem to begrudge paying this money, somehow assuming that the contribution of their spouse was insignificant.

Likewise, in relationships with families it is often easy to think that the partner looking after the kids has somehow got an easier role to play or that they don't really contribute to the overall success of the business.

I think that it is very important to stop and take stock of the role your partner plays in keeping your business (and often you) going. It should be all about appreciation rather than resentment; positive rather than negative. The more positive the relationships in your life the better your life will be as a whole.

What can I do today?

Take a moment to think of what your day-to-day life would be like without support, encouragement and nurturing from your partner. Think about all of the little things they do for you. If you don't feel supported, nurtured and encouraged by your spouse, perhaps now is an excellent time to sit down and talk about how you feel. It will clear the air, and make you and probably them feel much better. Either way, the end result will be good for you and your balanced business life.

#93 Admitting we are out of control means we are weak — wrong

Although this will come as no surprise to female readers, we men are not good at saying we need help. For some strange reason we associate needing help with being weak, and in many ways this is our greatest collective failing.

The very real feeling of being overwhelmed, of being severely stressed, out of control, and so on can be dramatically reduced simply by talking about it and getting someone to help. I state quite emphatically that any business issue that you may face has certainly been faced by someone else and, in all likelihood, is a common situation that will be easy to resolve. But the first step is to put your hand up and say that you need help.

Smart and very successful business owners have no problem doing this. They are smart on two levels. First, they know when they need help and aren't afraid to ask for it; second, they know where to find the help they need, normally by asking other people.

A few years ago I ended up in some financial difficulty. I had not managed my business finances that well, I had lost control of the money coming in and going out, and had spent some money before it had come in (and the contracts didn't eventuate). This was a very serious situation and I was facing going broke—for most business owners the most serious of situations. It is embarrassing, it is scary and you feel that you can't talk to anyone about it because news will get out and your customers will be afraid to deal with you.

Luckily, a good friend sensed that something was wrong. He sat me down, asked what was going on and I blurted it all out. He was fantastic—very rational and unemotional. In his own right he was a very successful and wealthy man, and he helped me to stop being emotional about the situation and to start being practical. My business was solid, there were plenty of customers coming through the door, but I was in the midst of a cashflow crunch, a very common problem for most small businesses (and many large ones). My friend simply showed me how to prioritise my payments, who to talk to about extending terms, how to approach slow-paying customers to get them to pay faster, and a host of other small and very achievable changes to what I was doing. Within a month I was well and truly back on track.

Now whenever I have a business issue that is stressing me out and causing me grief I don't hesitate to get help. I am always completely open and honest, I explain my situation fully, and once I get the advice I take it. This is so much better than stewing on it for months as things get worse and the situation goes from an irritation to a major problem.

So where do you get help? There are so many places it is hard to know where to start here. I recommend business mentors or people you know and respect, especially those who have been in business for a while. There are also government organisations everywhere that can point you in the right direction, as well as accountants, business coaches and business groups, to mention a few.

What can I do today?

Do you have any issues, business or otherwise, that you feel too embarrassed to talk about because you feel that others will think less of you? Find the right people to get help from and ask them to guide you through these tough times—but do it fast. The sooner you address a problem the better it will be for you because, generally, the easier it will be to fix.

#94 Treat your body as your most important business asset

I think our bodies should be included on our business balance sheet, that our health and wellbeing should be a legitimate expense. For many years I believed that the more work you put into your business the more successful it would be. I don't necessarily agree with that concept any more. Today I believe that the more work you put into yourself the more successful your business will be.

It is all about creating a healthy, successful, energetic person who is an entrepreneur. The by-product of this will be a host of successful small businesses (or large empires).

If we spent as much time and energy on our health and wellbeing as we do on our retirement, we would arrive at 65 in much better shape and with much more wealth.

Looking at your body as a business asset is an interesting and powerful way to realise that without good health your business will most likely fail anyway. So the healthier you are the healthier your business will be.

Put your body at the top of your list of assets. Feed it well, exercise it, treat it with respect and challenge it. Then enjoy what it brings you.

What can I do today?

There are many suggestions in this book on ways of improving your overall health and wellbeing. From my experience a large proportion of small business owners treat themselves poorly. Change this today and you will reap enormous rewards in the future.

Action page—What I need to do to regain balance in my life

----

12 | Balancing tips specifically for women

The tips in this section were given to me by a number of women who run their own businesses and still manage to have a life. I consulted a diverse group of women with businesses in fields ranging from chiropractic, aviation, fitness, tourism, legal and travel to accounting, restaurants, motivational speaking and publishing. They are a highly successful bunch, but like most small business owners they have all struggled with balance. I'd like to thank them for sharing their experience and suggestions (if anyone has any other tips that they would like to share please email me at ag@themarketingprofessionals.com.au).

And for the men sneaking a peek, some of these ideas may work just as well for you.

#95 Accept you are human and there are limits to what you can or should do
#96 Put yourself first every once in a while
#97 Don't compare yourself to others
#98 Allocate time with the girls
#99 Remember to live in the moment
#100 Stop worrying
#101 Do things to stimulate you as a woman

#95 Accept you are human and there are limits to what you can or should do

Women who balance a business and a family are truly amazing. I can only look on in awe. I have a friend who has three kids and her own business, and her husband has a business as well. They work really hard and at times it is tough going. But they just seem to get everything done, and they are good people who are active in the community, great parents, supportive friends and run successful businesses.

I meet a lot of women in similar situations, and what surprises me is that they are often really hard on themselves. They feel guilty for not spending enough time with the children or for not being better wives. It breaks my heart a little each time I hear this because I can see a human being who is really participating fully in life and doing a magnificent job, often contributing far more to the world than people with an abundance of time and/or money.

Many women have such high expectations of themselves they can only ever feel disappointed and guilty. They are trying to be Superwoman—a tough role to fill when they are merely human like the rest of us.

So my advice to all of the superwomen out there—every once in a while it is OK to wear a cape with wrinkles in it. It is OK if the house is a little (or a lot) messy or the kids have to sort out dinner for themselves. Aiming to be perfect all the time is an impossible expectation to live up to and a tough one for those around you to watch.

Now, it's very easy to tell someone to stop being hard on themselves, but it's often not that easy to actually stop doing it. I am not suggesting that you throw away this sense of duty and responsibility, just that you stop it from ruling your life, if in fact it does. One very effective way to change long-term habits is to start implementing small changes, one at a time. This may be as simple as learning to say no to things that you don't want to do, asking your family for help to get things done, or giving more responsibility to the people who work for you and letting them do it. In fact many of the tips in this book revolve around this concept of letting go, delegating, saying no, removing mounting responsibilities, and so on.

Sometimes it is a simply a matter of surrendering. Really, what is the problem if you don't get everything done on your list? How bad is it? Every once in a while we should just say 'that's it'—switch off the phone, tell everyone you are out of touch for the day and just be human. It isn't easy, but in the end the result is a much more relaxed, calm and happy person, and that is definitely the type of person who can run a profitable, successful business.

As an added bonus, I have found that the more you let the people around you take control the more they will—so let them. If they can share some of the responsibilities you struggle with, why not? Keep an eye on them, support them, ensure they are not getting overwhelmed themselves, but let them go for it.

What can I do today?

Superwomen—have a day off and just be you, warts and all. Your business will be better off as a result. In fact, you might be surprised by how smoothly things continue to run without you.

#96 Put yourself first every once in a while

Not only should you have a break from being Superwoman every once in a while, but how about going one step further and putting yourself first occasionally as well?

Women, especially mothers, often fall into a habit of always putting others before themselves. This approach then carries over into the way they run their businesses. Everyone else gets looked after except the woman in charge. While it is very noble, it is also very stressful, particularly as the business grows and all of a sudden you are 'mother' to more and more people.

The first step of this process is understanding and believing in the importance of putting yourself first. Sure, there are times when this is impractical, and no one likes a completely self-centred person. I am not suggesting that is what you should become. But what I see is too many women in business who always put themselves last—in everything they do. Some people may think of putting yourself first as being selfish, but it is really to do with self-respect. If you are OK, everyone around you will be more OK than if you are not. There are times when we all get pushed into doing things that we don't want to do. We are 'guilted' into them, made to feel responsible for an outcome, or as though it would be irresponsible not to do what is expected of us.

Well, sometimes you have to take a stand and say that enough is enough. One simple example of this is to pay yourself first every week. Most business owners pay themselves last; it's a habit we get into. Change this habit, if nothing else, and reward yourself for all that you do by paying yourself first. What is left over can then be put into the pot of bills that need to be paid, and if you are a little short that week, someone else will just have to wait. Running a business can be a thankless task, and you are in the courageous minority for doing it in the first place. Reward yourself for being brave enough to have a go.

What can I do today?

Next time you find yourself ignoring your own needs and putting someone else first, stop, take a moment and think about this self-sacrifice. Are you doing it because you really want to and it's the right thing to do in this situation, or are you doing it because you always do it? Buy some time before committing to your next responsibility—tell the person you need to check a few things and you will get back to them. Slow the process down and give yourself enough time to evaluate your decision-making process and course of action.

#97 Don't compare yourself to others

Sometimes it feels as though everyone else is making more money, getting more accolades, bringing up their children better, that they are skinnier, better dressed, more interesting, with better looking husbands and more exciting lives. It's easy to start making comparisons—'She's the same age as I am, in business for herself like me, but her life seems to be running much more smoothly than mine and she is clearly making much more money than me.'

Now, I cannot overemphasise how dangerous it is to compare where you are in life with those around you. For starters, everyone else's business will look better than yours at some stage. I often find myself daydreaming about running every kind of business imaginable, and on some days (clearly when I am temporarily insane) I think how much easier it would be to run a different kind of business, say a retail shop or, even better, a restaurant. Now, I know for a fact that both of these are really, really tough businesses to run and to be successful in, yet at times I can't help but feel they must be easier than mine. Take it from me, having dealt with thousands upon thousands of business owners through my books, seminars, consulting, training and coaching I now know that there is no such thing as the perfect business. Every business has its challenges.

With regard to success, looks can be deceiving. Just because someone drives a BMW doesn't necessarily mean they are really successful; frequently it means they just have a lot of debt. But let's say you meet a business owner who *is* really successful financially. Rather than comparing yourself with them and feeling that you fall short of their achievements, why not learn from them and their successes. Good on them, they have worked hard and probably faced many of the same challenges you have had to deal with.

It is easy to compare yourself to others and feel that you come up short. In fact it is really easy because there are so many amazing people in the world. But my guess is you are amazing, too, in your own way. Take stock of what you have achieved, what you have acquired and what your successes are, and appreciate them. Use heroes and idols to drive you forward but not to make you envious of their successes.

From time to time we all get caught in a deep, dark hole of self-doubt. Comparing where you are in life to other people is natural, but learn to accept it as a passing phase, not a permanent reflection of your life. At times like this try not to think about what you don't have; instead think about what you do have. A very good friend of mine, Andrew Matthews, writes truly amazing books about what sounds like a very simple topic—being happy. He has sold millions of copies around the world. I strongly recommend investing in any of his excellent books.

What can I do today?

Go out and buy a copy of Andrew Matthews's very entertaining and powerful book *Being Happy*. It explains in very simple terms, with the use of delightful cartoons, why comparing where you are in life with other people is a waste of your time and energy.

#98 Allocate time with the girls

There is nothing like spending some time with your closest friends, away from the demands of the business, the family and everything in between. Sometimes nothing helps to get rid of stress and clutter better than a night out with the girls.

Like many of the things that keep your life in balance, time spent on yourself is one of the first things to go as everyday responsibilities build up.

Spending time with friends is incredibly restorative, especially if they are not involved in your business. You can complain, moan, get things off your chest and not be judged. Sometimes you just need to purge. At other times you might be the one offering support to your friends; this is equally powerful because it gets you out of your own head for a while. And celebrating our successes is much more enjoyable when we do it with those people who really appreciate and understand what we had to do to achieve these results.

If your business has taken over your life and you have lost touch with your girlfriends, now is the time to start rebuilding those bridges. Spend some time doing what you enjoy, even if it is only a short catch-up over a coffee. You will feel much better in many ways.

What can I do today?

Send out an email or call up your closest friends and arrange a get-together. If they aren't close by, arrange a teleconference or a webcam. Everyone can ring in and you can chat away for hours. This can be lots of fun and is a convenient and inexpensive way to keep in touch.

#99 Remember to live in the moment

Trying to fit everything into our busy lives, we spend a lot of time and energy planning, thinking about the future, booking appointments, managing relationships, doing our work, and meeting every other obligation and task that we need to do. The more responsibilities you have the more structure and forward planning you need to make it all work. It's a simple fact of life.

It's no wonder that many of us have forgotten how to stop and enjoy the moment, right here, right now. Living your entire life checking your watch, your diary and talking on your mobile phone, you are always looking ahead and forgetting what is happening right in front of you.

Stop every now and then to smell the roses and to celebrate victories, large and small. Why not send a thankyou note, or just pause to appreciate what you have achieved and what you have.

Many of the offices in my building have amazing views over the ocean. When I have meetings with people who are lucky enough to have these views I often comment on how spectacular they are, and it is interesting how frequently these people look out the window like it is the first time they have noticed the beautiful scenery. Often they make the comment that they rarely even look out the window anymore. How sad is that? We all face the same challenge on a day-to-day basis, in business and in life.

Women with families and businesses are the busiest people on the planet; all the more reason to stop every now and then and look at the view. You earned it, and you deserve to enjoy it.

What can I do today?

Spend a few minutes thinking about all of the wonderful things in your life, what you have achieved so far and what you are grateful for. Try to do this whenever you are feeling a little lost or overwhelmed.

#100 Stop worrying

It's an interesting thing, worrying. Most of the things we worry about never occur. In fact, some statistics say that as much as 90 per cent of what we worry about will never happen. So why do we spend so much time and energy on things we can't change?

I do know that some people worry a lot more than others. I also think that generally women worry more than men. While I can't really explain why we worry, I can give ways to ease the pain associated with worry.

I was a worrier for many years, but in the end I got exhausted from so much worrying and now I don't do it so much. Here are ten of my favourite tips for overcoming worry:

1. Decide what is the very worst that can happen and think about what this would mean for you. Is it really that bad? Are there any good things that might come out of it?
2. Don't hide from problems. Confront them head on, no matter how uncomfortable this may be. The sooner you acknowledge the problem the sooner it will be resolved.
3. Talk to people you trust. When we are really worried about something we often feel very alone. Sharing it really does help, and all of a sudden the clouds don't look quite so dark and foreboding.
4. Get professional help. There is someone out there who can help to resolve just about any issue you may have. It's just a matter of tracking them down. Don't wait too long to get help.
5. If the issue is too much to deal with as a whole, see if you can break it down into smaller parts that you *can* cope with.
6. Be open and honest with yourself and others—the more honest you are the less there is to worry about.

7. Let go of ego. It is ego that makes you worry about what you might lose and what other people will think of you, and it feeds the worry bug.

8. When you find yourself worrying about a situation, try to distance yourself from it. Imagine if a friend came to you with the same issue: what advice would you give them? Why is it different for you?

9. There are times to worry and times not to worry. Save your energy for things that really matter—such as issues of life and death. Give yourself a little reality check every once in a while.

10. Sometimes we worry incessantly about an issue for weeks, months and even years. It's often better to just make a decision. Right or wrong, who cares? You can always make another decision down the track. Decide so that you can move forward rather than remaining in a stale-mate situation.

I hope these tips will help you to overcome worry in the future. Remember, if you've got a problem—front it.

What can I do today?

Stop worrying and start living. If you are worrying about something right now, read through my list of ways to overcome worry and solve the problem today.

#101 Do things to stimulate you as a woman

Just as men need to do the things that stimulate them (stand around a BBQ and talk about sport, watch sport, play sport, read about sport and then talk about sport some more), it is just as important for women to do things that stimulate the feminine energy in their life.

In doing my own survey on this I heard a great variety of suggestions. Some women love to climb mountains, some shop, some are big on renovations. For some it is being creative and painting, while others love camping or seeing a movie, and some love cooking and baking. Whatever it is that rocks your boat, it doesn't matter. The important message is really to embrace being a woman and do the things that stimulate you.

Business can be quite a male-dominated world. It can be challenging, it can be sexist and it can be aggressive. Many women (and men) find this difficult. There is a real need to balance this strong male energy with a more tempered and nurturing female energy. The best way to do this is to find the time to do the things that feed your female energy. Look at it as a rebalancing exercise.

Decide what you most enjoy doing with your spare time and make sure you do it as often as you can, either alone or with friends. You will be much better equipped to deal with the stress and negative energy you may encounter in your business life.

What can I do today?

Be clear on what nurtures you as a woman and aim to do it more often. This is your time: make sure you indulge yourself, and don't waste any time feeling guilty.

221

Action page—What I need to do to regain balance in my life

----

20 bonus tips that will help right now

The following quick tips are designed to be used right now if you are in the middle of an attack of feeling overwhelmed. They only take a few seconds to read and a few seconds to action. There are bound to be one or two that will resonate with you right away.

Bonus tip #1 Close your door

We all need to regain some composure from time to time. A few simple minutes away from the madding crowds and the stress and pressure associated with work can do it for most of us. Train your staff to understand that if your door is shut they don't interrupt you unless it is an emergency. This will give you a sense of safety and protection in your workplace, and a few precious moments to just stop and think about what is happening.

Bonus tip #2 Shut your eyes and take a few deep breaths

When faced with the feeling that the walls are closing in, which can be caused by too much information for the brain to process, closing your eyes and taking ten deep breaths can help to restore calm in a very short period of time. The less external stimulation you have the better. Find a quiet place, get comfortable, close your eyes and make those breaths long, slow and deep. 'Take ten' as often as you need to.

Bonus tip #3 Ring a friend who always calms you down

We all have someone whose very voice seems to calm us down. They accept us the way we are, they don't judge us or what we do. They simply understand us. Use this person in times of need. Call them, tell them how you are feeling and simply communicate. It is very therapeutic to just talk through a feeling of being overwhelmed—and often just getting it off your chest seems to make it go away.

Bonus tip #4 Establish priorities—what has to be done now?

Another problem with feeling out of control is that we tend to 'freeze'—we stop everything because we don't know what to do next. The tasks seem to have piled up and more just keep getting added. One of the best things you can do here is to make a list of everything you need to do. This is a great starting point because the information stops floating chaotically around inside your head and instead is set out in black and white in front of you. Once you have the list, allocate priorities—urgent, not so urgent, kind of urgent, a bit urgent, bugger it (or something like that). All of a sudden, the overwhelming feeling of all of these tasks needing to be done becomes a little less daunting, as quite often you realise that things aren't as bad as you thought they were.

Bonus tip #5 Have two big glasses of cold water

In times of stress we tend to reach for things that stress us out even more—coffee, tea, sugar, cigarettes, alcohol. While there is a short-term calming or comforting effect associated with these chemicals, longer term they make things worse. Most of us can relate to the craving for caffeine, closely followed by the jitters after having had too much coffee. Try to retrain yourself to have not one but two big glasses of cold water whenever you are feeling stressed out or overwhelmed. The craving for a stimulant normally goes, and in the longer term (the next few hours) you will feel much calmer and better able to cope.

Bonus tip #6 Ask for help from those around you

Let everyone close to you know exactly how you are feeling. Get the troops to rally around the flag and let them know how they can help you to get through this overwhelming situation. Sharing the stress, the demands, the tension will help it to dissipate and let you get on with regaining composure and calm.

Bonus tip #7 See a movie

As hard as it is to get ourselves out of the situation that is overwhelming us, that is exactly what we need to do. Why don't you go to a movie—it gives your brain time to relax and process, and you get to sit in a cool, dark room, hopefully while being entertained and enthralled. There are no other demands on you—all you have to do is sit.

Bonus tip #8 Remember to be grateful for being busy

Often we look at these periods of craziness in the wrong light. Really, in light of the number of businesses that go broke every day in every city in the world, we should be grateful to be full-on and under pressure to deliver. Of course, there are times when the money is tight and that is why we are under the hammer and feeling overwhelmed, but, from experience, things can always be worse. Taking a moment to be grateful for what we do have rather than what we don't have is a powerful way to battle being stressed out and overwhelmed.

Bonus tip #9 Start saying no right now

One of the greatest causes of becoming overwhelmed is the inability to say no. Perhaps there are certain tasks or demands on you that you could say no to right now and make your life easier. The habit of saying yes all the time out of fear of losing customers is a good habit to break. If meeting the deadline set by a customer will really stress you out and cause you to become overwhelmed, say no. OK—you might lose a customer here or there, but do you really want them if they won't work with you?

Bonus tip #10 Wipe your diary clean until you get on top of things

One practice used by many business owners in times of stress is to cancel all appointments and meetings until they have got things back under control. While this may sound a little drastic, it is a very effective way to get some space to think and to manage your way through a stressful time. It lets you deal with the issues in front of you without others being added to the pile.

Bonus tip #11 What is the very worst that can happen?

There is a wonderful book written by Dale Carnegie called *How to Stop Worrying and Start Living*. Like his very famous

How to Win Friends and Influence People, it was written over 60 years ago, but the very practical advice it contains about managing worry is just as relevant today as it was then. One of Carnegie's key points was to imagine the very worst that can happen in any situation, then think it through and accept it. Most of what we worry about will never, ever happen, but if we imagine the worst, then accept that if it happens we will survive and move on, the threat and power of the situation is easier to deal with.

Bonus tip #12 Get out of your environment

Going to the movies was suggested in bonus tip #7, to give you time to process the stress and to calm down. If that isn't practical, just getting out of your work environment will help. It might just take a walk around the block. Get out, calm down, get your head together and come back when you are feeling better equipped to deal with what is happening. When the going gets tough—get out of there!

Bonus tip #13 Restrict communication to the essentials if you can

Often the biggest issue in those out-of-control times is that you don't get a chance to take a breath. It might be a never-ending stream of telephone calls, customers or staff coming through the door. If possible, let everyone know that you need some time to manage a very important matter and to please hold all calls or interruptions unless they're urgent. Spell it out—try to restrict the information coming through so you get a chance to collect your thoughts and regroup. Turn your mobile phone off, avoid checking your email, shut your door—do whatever it takes to give yourself breathing space.

Bonus tip #14 Take a long, hot shower

Not the easiest thing to do in most workplaces, but a long, hot shower is very calming and relaxing if you can make it happen. There are a number of places away from home where you can have a shower—health clubs, transit centres, hotels, sports centres, etc. Taking the time to indulge in a luxurious shower is an excellent investment in your own wellbeing in times of stress and it will definitely help to calm you down. You just need to be a little organised to do it.

Bonus tip #15 Have a big stretch (it really does help)

Stretching is very therapeutic. Stress makes us tense up, hunch our back and shoulders, and generally get 'smaller'. Doing some simple stretching, especially of the bigger muscles in your chest, back and legs, will make you feel much better. Do the stretch and hold it to get the best effect. You don't need to be able to turn yourself into a pretzel to benefit from stretching— all you need is some room to move, a wall to lean against or a patch of floor to lie down on (and, if you are lucky, grab a few minutes' sleep while you are there).

Bonus tip #16 Eat a good meal (but not a heavy meal)

Another problem associated with the out-of-control phase is that we don't tend to stop and eat a proper meal. Instead we eat on the run, generally choosing food that is fast and filling rather than nutritious. Taking the time to order a good meal, but not one that is overly heavy, and then sitting down to enjoy it in a peaceful, relaxing environment is an excellent way to calm down. In many parts of the world this is a ritual—and for good reason. Ideally, follow this meal with an afternoon siesta and you will feel fantastic. Well OK—the afternoon sleep might be a little much to ask, but at least try the meal.

Bonus tip #17 Get yourself a massage

For people who are really busy, stressed out and starting to feel totally out of control, sitting still is hard enough, let alone lying down and getting a massage. But it is incredible how wonderful and recharged a good massage can make you feel. All it takes is one hour (anything less is not enough). For those of us who lead constantly stressful lives, building in time for a massage every single week should be a priority, and one that will certainly pay off in every way.

Bonus tip #18 Write down exactly how you are feeling

Often it is hard to pinpoint exactly what it is that has made you feel overwhelmed. Is it a sense of never getting on top of things? Do you feel scared that you will go broke if you don't get everything done? Are you worried about keeping good staff? Do you really think that you are not capable of running your own business? This is deep stuff, but if you can hit the nail on the head as to why you are feeling over-whelmed it tends to defuse the situation and you will feel much better.

Bonus tip #19 Break down what you need to do into small steps and bite-size chunks

We tend to freeze when we feel overwhelmed. You might have made a list of everything that you need to do and prioritised these tasks (as per bonus tip #4), but sometimes you need that extra bit of help to get started. Every task, project and action can generally be broken down into smaller, more manageable parts—just a small step in the right direction will help the rising panic and overwhelming feelings pass.

Bonus tip #20 Try to see the funny side

If you have picked up only one good tip from this book, I certainly hope it is about having fun in your business. For some wonderful reason, a good belly laugh can do more to relieve stress and overcome feelings of being overwhelmed than hours of meditation or sleep. There are very few situations that are really that bad—after all, it is only business.

Where to from here?

The battle for balance is here to stay, at least for a while. It is unlikely that any of us can be cured overnight, but the ideas, recommendations and philosophies covered in this book, if applied, will most certainly help.

They are based on tried and tested techniques from people who have faced and continue to face this ongoing challenge every day. Owning and operating your own business should be a wonderful experience. It should be rewarding, challenging, exciting and lucrative. For it to be all of these things we need to work out what level of balance we are after and what we have to do to achieve it.

I truly hope that this book has helped you. I also recommend that you keep it handy and dip into it often, as different sections will have different meanings and interpretations in the various stages of your life.

Appendix: Blank forms to help you regain balance

These forms are designed to help you achieve your balance. Feel free to copy them, distribute them, cut them out and generally use them anywhere you can.

- Your business–life balance questionnaire
- Remember the things you really enjoy doing
- Your accomplishments
- Identify what stresses you out the most
- Your ideal life
- The top ten changes you need to make
- What goes into your body?

Your business–life balance questionnaire

Simply put a tick for yes next to the questions that you feel apply to you and how you are feeling now. Then tally up the ticks and see the results (refer to pages 3–4 for an explanation of scores). Each time you fill in this form, compare the number of ticks with your previous results so that you can track your progress.

How balanced is your life?

☐ Do you feel that you never have enough time to get everything done?

☐ Do you feel that your decision-making is always done under pressure?

☐ Are there times during your day when you feel totally overwhelmed or out of control?

☐ Do you think that stress is affecting your health?

☐ Do you always feel low in energy?

☐ Do you use drugs or alcohol to help you wind down?

☐ Do you use caffeine and sugar to help you wind up?

☐ Do you tend to eat foods that will give you a 'quick fix' rather than foods that are healthy and nutritious?

☐ Are you working longer and longer hours?

☐ Do you struggle to find the time to exercise?

☐ Have you stopped spending quality time with family and friends since starting or buying your own business?

☐ Have you stopped doing the things you love (hobbies, sport, etc.)?

☐ Do you tend to get sick more often or do you always feel off-colour/below par?

☐ Have you lost your sense of satisfaction with your business?

☐ Do you tend to keep your thoughts and emotions to yourself?

☐ Do you lose sleep worrying about business issues?

☐ Do you struggle financially?

☐ Has your personality changed (for the worse) since you've been in business?

☐ Have you stopped enjoying life as much as you did before?

☐ Are you feeling uninspired?

☐ Do you consider your time at home as being predominantly to recharge and prepare for the next day?

☐ Do you tend to feel negative more often than positive?

☐ Are you more grumpy and irritable now?

☐ Do you bring work home with you?

☐ Is every day starting to look the same?

☐ Do you have a lot of negative people in your life?

☐ Are you feeling depressed?

☐ Do you have a large number of unfinished tasks?

☐ Has your overall fitness level dropped in recent years?

☐ Have people stopped telling you that you look well?

☐ Do you sometimes feel like crying?

Total

Remember the things you really enjoy doing

The aim of this exercise is to make a list of the things you used to do which you really enjoyed doing. Then write down the last time you did them and, most importantly, when you will do them next. This page should be copied and put in a prominent place!

	Activity	Last time you did it	When will you do it next?
1			
2			
3			
4			
5			
6			
7			
8			
9			
10			

Your accomplishments

This page is all about what you have achieved in your life. Take a few moments to fill as many spaces as you can with all your achievements—no matter how big or small, they all count.

Example: Learned to roller skate—age six

Identify what stresses you out the most

Take a few moments to really identify exactly what it is that causes you to feel stressed out and overwhelmed. Be specific and try to determine not so much the action but rather the underlying reason why it affects you.

This stresses me out a lot	Why?
Example: People come into my office	I never get anything done because I am always being interrupted.

Your ideal life

This is really more of a creative writing session. Take a few moments to write down exactly how you would like your life to be. Be specific, identify figures, names, activities, etc. The aim is to create a picture of what the life you would like to lead really looks like—by doing this, you will be starting on the journey to making it a reality.

My ideal life is . . .

The top ten changes you need to make

Choose the ten tips recommended in this book that you think will make the greatest impact on you and help you to regain control of your business and your life. Allot a realistic deadline to each one and then turn them into reality. Remember, if you always do what you always did, you will always get what you've always got.

	Top ten tips to help restore balance	Due date
1		
2		
3		
4		
5		
6		
7		
8		
9		
10		

Copyright © Andrew Griffiths 2007. This template may be photocopied for non-commercial use.

What goes into your body?

In this chart, establish what you eat and drink when you are feeling stressed out and, ideally, what you could replace any negatives with. Clearly it is hard to make a dramatic change, especially when most of the food and drink which is not that good for us is so readily available. But persevere, try it for a week and see how it makes you feel.

	Food/drink type	Where	When	Feeling	Replace it with
1	Example: Coffee	Home	Morning	To get started	Fresh juice
2					
3					
4					
5					
6					
7					

	Food/drink type	Where	When	Feeling	Replace it with
8					
9					
10					
11	Example: Chocolate bar	Office	Between 3–4 pm daily	Brief energy burst	Fruit and nuts
12					
13					
14					

Recommended reading and websites

Allardice, P., 2006, *Slow Up*, Allen & Unwin, Sydney.

Breitman, P. and Hatch, C., 2000, *How to Say No Without Feeling Guilty*, Broadway Books, New York.

Canfield, J. and Switzer, J., 2005, *The Success Principles: How to get from where you are to where you want to be*, Harper-Collins, USA.

Carlson, R., 1997, *Don't Sweat the Small Stuff*, Hyperion, New York.

——1998, *You Can Be Happy No Matter What*, New World Library, California.

Carnegie, D., 1981, *How to Win Friends and Influence People*, HarperCollins, New York.

——1985, *How to Stop Worrying and Start Living*, Pocket Books (a division of Simon & Schuster), New York.

Chin-Ning, C., 1998, *Do Less, Achieve More*, Regan Books, New York.

Covey, S., 2004, *The 8th Habit—from effectiveness to greatness*, Free Press (a division of Simon & Schuster), New York.

Cowley, J., 2003, *I Need Balance in My Life*, Richmond Ventures, Sydney.

Gerrish, R. and Leader, S., 2005, *Flying Solo*, Allen & Unwin, Sydney.

Grieve, T., 2004, *The book for people who do too much*, Random House, Sydney.

Herald, J., 2006, *What are you waiting for? If nothing changes nothing changes*, Allen & Unwin, Sydney.

Lundin, S., Paul, H. and Christensen, J., 2002, *Fish! Tales: Real-Life Stories to Help You Transform Your Workplace and Your Life*, Hyperion Publishing, New York.

Matthews, A., 1998, *Being Happy*, Media Masters, Singapore.

———2005, *Happiness Now*, Seashell Publishers, Australia.

Morgenstern, J., 2000, *Time management from the inside out*, Henry Holt and Company, New York.

Tolle, E., 2004, *The Power of Now*, Hodder, Sydney.

Wilson, P., 2005, *Perfect Balance: Create time and space for all parts of your life*, Penguin Books, Melbourne.

Websites

The following websites will provide you with ideas and suggestions to improve your business as well as meet the challenge of balancing your business and your life.

www.flyingsolo.com.au
www.andrewgriffiths.com.au
www.lifebydesign.com.au
www.business.gov.au
www.smallbusiness.com
www.entrepreneur.com
www.smallbusiness.co.uk
www.ivillage.co.uk

About the author

Andrew Griffiths is an entrepreneur with a passion for small business. From humble beginnings as an orphan growing up in Western Australia, Andrew has owned and operated a number of successful small businesses, with his first enterprise—at age seven—being a paper round. Since then, he has sold encyclopaedias door to door, travelled the world as an international sales manager, worked in the Great Sandy Desert for a gold exploration company and been a commercial diver. Clearly this unusual combination of experiences has made him the remarkable man he is.

Inspired by his constant desire to see others reach their goals, Andrew has written five hugely successful books, with many more on the way. His *101 Ways* series offers small business owners practical, passionate and achievable advice. The series is sold in over 40 countries worldwide.

Andrew is the founding director of **The Marketing Professionals**, one of Australia's best and most respected strategic marketing and corporate imaging firms.

Known for his ability to entertain, inspire and deliver key messages, Andrew is also a powerful keynote presenter, who brings flamboyant energy and verve to the corporate world.

All of this occurs from his chosen home of Cairns, North Queensland, the Great Barrier Reef, Australia.

To find out more about Andrew Griffiths please visit the following websites:

www.andrewgriffiths.com.au
www.themarketingprofessionals.com
www.enhanceplus.com.au
www.allenandunwin.com

101 WAYS TO MARKET YOUR BUSINESS

Stand out from the crowd.

Here are 101 practical marketing suggestions to help you achieve dramatic improvements in your business without investing a lot of time and money.

Simple, affordable and quick, these innovative tips are easy to implement and will bring you fast results. Choose and apply at least one new idea each week or use this book as a source of inspiration for new ways to market your services, your products and your business itself.

With tips that take just a few moments to read, *101 Ways to Market Your Business* will help you find new customers, increase the loyalty of the customers you already have, create great promotional material and make your business stand out from the crowd.

INCLUDES 20 BONUS SUGGESTIONS TO HELP YOU ATTRACT NEW CUSTOMERS AND KEEP YOUR EXISTING ONES

101 WAYS TO ADVERTISE YOUR BUSINESS

Read this before you spend another cent on advertising.

Here are 101 proven tips to increase the effectiveness of your advertising. Use these tips to understand what makes one ad work while another fails and you will save a small fortune in wasted advertising.

With tips that take just a few moments to read, *101 Ways to Advertise Your Business* offers step-by-step advice on how to make an advertisement, how to buy advertising space and how to ensure that your advertisement is working to its full potential. Follow the tips and your business will soon be reaping the benefits.

INCLUDES A SPECIAL BONUS SECTION CONTAIN-ING HUNDREDS OF THE BEST ADVERTISING WORDS AND PHRASES

101 WAYS TO REALLY SATISFY YOUR CUSTOMERS

Simple ways to keep your customers coming back.

Here are 101 practical tips for delivering service that exceeds your customers' expectations and keeps them coming back. In a world where consumers are far more informed, discerning and demanding than ever before, customer service is one of the main areas where a business can outshine its competitors.

Use these simple tips to improve your customer service and you will be well on the way to success and profitability. With tips that take just a few moments to read, *101 Ways to Really Satisfy Your Customers* teaches you to identify what customers expect, and details simple suggestions that will enable your business to exceed these expectations and reap the rewards.

INCLUDES 20 BONUS TIPS THAT WILL REALLY IMPRESS YOUR CUSTOMERS